P9-DBP-547

Queen Victoria

This is the romantic story of a queen's heart and a nation's destiny, and of the fierce conflict between love and duty. A queen at eighteen, Victoria displayed an amazing maturity in her understanding of her overwhelming responsibilities. Her marriage to her German cousin, Prince Albert, changed her from an imperious monarch to a humble adoring wife. During twenty-one happy years they raised nine children. When Albert died, Victoria went into complete mourning, evading her responsibilities. But her people soon made her realize that her personal life was secondary to her role as Queen. Victoria's 60th year on the throne was celebrated as a Diamond Jubilee and she was universally mourned when she died at eighty-two.

Queen Victoria

(May 24, 1819 – January 22, 1901)

by Molly Costain Haycraft

JULIAN MESSNER, INC. NEW YORK

Published by Julian Messner, Inc.
8 West 40th Street, New York 18
Published simultaneously in Canada
By the Copp Clark Company, Ltd.

Library of Congress Catalog Card No. 56-6788

Printed in the United States of America

Fourth Printing, 1963

For
My Mother

Contents

Queen Victoria

King George III and Queen Charlotte

George IV
Charlotte

Frederick
Duke of York

William IV
Duke of Clarence

Edward
Duke of Kent

Ernest
Duke of Cumberland

Augustus
Duke of Sussex

Adolphus
Duke of Cambridge

I

A Queen Is Born

Victoria walked briskly into the schoolroom and settled down at her desk, quite ready to begin the day's work. Although she was only eleven she was naturally industrious and, as she had always been taught right here at home in the familiar rooms of Kensington Palace, she had no reason to dread her lessons. Her only teachers so far had been her governess Lehzen and now her dear Mr. Davys, who made everything so interesting.

She took out her preparation for this particular day in the year 1830 and glanced over it. Mr. Davys had set her a rather unusual task, but she was pretty sure it was correctly done. "Make me a neatly written chart of the kings and queens of England," he had said to her, "showing how the line of succession goes." Here it was, free of blots, on a good sheet of parchment.

Mr. Davys, who had been busy at his table, now looked up. "Bring me your work, please, Victoria."

A few minutes later he carried the chart back to her

desk and stood, for a moment, looking down at the young girl with her head bent over her book. It was a pretty head, with light hair neatly arranged in ringlets, and when she smiled up at him he thought, as he often did, how much she reminded him of a little bird. She was small for her age and the bright eyes, the quickness of her glance, something about the expression of the prim, tiny mouth, all were robinlike, although he had to admit he had never seen a blue-eyed robin!

"It is correct, Victoria," he said, "as far as you have gone. You have stopped here with your Uncle Billy and you haven't put down the next heir to the throne."

Victoria sat quietly, her cheeks turning a bit pinker than they were before. "I—" she hesitated. "I hardly liked to put down myself."

Although she may not have realized it, this was an important moment in her life. Until this very day her mother and everyone else around her had tried to keep from her the fact that she would probably wear the crown of England. As much as possible, they wanted her to enjoy the life of a normal girl. But now she had to know, for it was time for her to take her place as the acknowledged heir to the throne. It would mean, even now, certain public duties and honors and she must apply herself, from now on, even harder to all the lessons put before her. It meant that, young as she was, she must guard her every word and deed; she must say and do nothing unfitting to her high position.

However, as her answer to Mr. Davys showed, she

knew her future already. The truth had come to her gradually and she thought about it a great deal. Some of her thoughts had been sad ones, because even at eleven, and without discussing the matter with anyone, she knew that to be a queen was not just to sit on a golden throne with a glittering crown on her head. She had even cried a bit when no one was looking.

Now she could talk about it. She put out her hand to Mr. Davys, who took it and held it comfortingly. She said, very seriously, "I will be good."

Our story could start here, but there is really another beginning.

Back in 1817 the Duke of Kent, Victoria's father, learned of the death of his niece, Princess Charlotte. And that is the day the story should begin—because if Princess Charlotte had not died, Victoria would never have been born.

Princess Charlotte's father was the direct heir to the throne of England. Her grandfather was George III, then king. Charlotte's father was George, the Prince of Wales, oldest son of George III, and she was his only child. This is the way the succession to the throne of England goes: when a king dies, his oldest son becomes king; then *his* oldest son becomes king after him. If a king has only a daughter, then she becomes queen. So it seemed clear that the crown would pass from George III to George IV to Charlotte and then to her oldest son, if she had one. She was young and happily married to

Leopold of Saxe-Coburg, later to become Leopold I, King of Belgium, and they were eagerly awaiting their first baby. But poor Leopold lost his wife and his baby and the Prince of Wales lost his only child.

When the direct heir to the throne is childless, the next in line after him is the king's next son. George III had six more sons and several daughters, but the daughters would not be in line to reign as long as there were any sons or any children of those sons still alive. So, after George III died, the crown would pass from brother to brother until it reached one with an heir, and then that heir would inherit it and keep it from going on to the next brother.

When Princess Charlotte died, Edward, the Duke of Kent, the fourth son of King George III, studied the same table of succession that his daughter would be learning thirteen years later. The Prince of Wales, whose only child had just died, was, even in 1817, an unhealthy, bloated man. He was separated from his wife and it was unlikely that he would ever be free to marry again and have more children.

Frederick, Duke of York, came next. He had no children and his marriage was obviously a barren one. William, Duke of Clarence, thinking himself far from the throne, had never made a royal marriage. Nor had Edward, Duke of Kent. Members of the royal family, unless they sign away all their rights to the throne, must have their marriages approved by the reigning monarch. This is called the Royal Marriage Act, and was put in force to prevent princes and princesses from marrying commoners and producing children ineligible to wear the crown.

So here was Edward, Duke of Kent, a bachelor of fifty-one, considering marriage. He had spent a great deal of his life doing military duty in Canada and Gibraltar and now, he felt, a new duty faced him. He must marry and produce an heir to the throne. Of course his greatest hope was to be king himself someday, but with three brothers ahead of him it was possible he might die before his turn came. However, if he had a child and they did not, his child would wear the crown of England when they died.

Whom should he marry? There were several possibilities, but his final choice was Victoire Marie Louise of Saxe-Coburg, Princess of Leiningen, sister of Charlotte's husband, Leopold. She was an attractive widow of about thirty who would be very acceptable under the Marriage Act and, as she had a son and daughter by her first husband, it seemed likely that she would have more children.

Edward Augustus took Victoire Marie Louise in the bonds of holy matrimony for the express purpose of having an heir; that same year his brothers William, the Duke of Clarence, and Adolphus, the Duke of Cambridge, both married for the same reason. Later that summer the Kents traveled to England to be remarried there and they went through a double wedding ceremony with the Clarences at Kew Palace.

The Prince of Wales was ruling England as Prince Regent at this time because his father, King George III, was mentally unbalanced. He knew why his brothers were all rushing to be married and the whole matter was so distasteful to him that he suggested they live abroad. This was agreeable to the Kents—for the time being, anyway—and they returned to Germany and settled down in Amorbach, a place they both liked very much. They were extremely happy together, and before long they knew that the much-desired baby was going to be born to them.

"I have been thinking," said Edward to his wife one afternoon, "that we should return to England. A child that may wear the crown of England should certainly be born there." He turned and looked out the window. "Unfortunately, I seem to be out of funds." This was always the case with the Duke of Kent, who could not seem to curb his extravagant tendencies. "But I will write my brother George and ask him for money for the trip and for the royal yacht to cross the Channel."

Edward could, of course, have arranged for himself and Victoire to travel from Germany to England, but as members of the royal family they had living with them what amounted to a little court—ladies and gentlemen, maids and lackies and, in this instance, Victoire's daughter, Feodore, and her governess. Her son, Charles, would remain in Germany as he was heir to the Duchy of Leiningen. Moving a household of this size was a problem and the Prince Regent refused to pay for it.

He had heard that William, the Duke of Clarence, was expecting a baby, too, and he resented the thought of these infants who were being born to take his place.

There is almost always someone who is happy to lend money to a prince and Edward soon found such a friend. After a bit of badgering, the Prince Regent agreed to send the yacht for them; so the Kents made all their final arrangements. The trunks were packed and off they went, the Duke and the Duchess, Feodore and her governess, maids, nurses, ladies, gentlemen and gentlemen's gentlemen, lapdogs and canaries.

Poor Victoire, not feeling too well anyway, found the hired carriage quite uncomfortable as it bounced over the rough roads. The inns were bad, too, and they had to stay in cheap ones, so it was not a pleasant trip for anyone; even the Channel crossing was unusually rough. However, they arrived safely in London at last and went immediately to Kensington Palace, where a set of rooms had been grudgingly allotted to them by the Prince of Wales.

They settled down to await their baby. William's child, they heard, had been born and had died. "I am not surprised," said Edward. "A gypsy in Gibraltar told me I would have a daughter who would be a great queen, and I am sure her prophecy is going to come true."

Victoire was delighted with her new home, for Kensington Palace is a beautiful old red brick building with rows of tall windows that let soft light into the large rooms and the long halls. Besides its suites of comfortable living quarters it has elaborate state chambers; for Kensington has been the home of many of England's kings and queens, including William and Mary, Anne, and George II. London surrounds it now; but its lovely gardens and parks and ponds were almost in the country then, and it was far enough from the center of things to make its inhabitants a bit nervous about coming home after dark. You never knew when a footpad would hold you up and take your purse and jewels.

May 24, 1819, a day which is now one of Great Britain's annual holidays, was just beginning. It was four o'clock in the morning and London was dark and quiet. But one corner of Kensington Palace was full of lights, people, and activity; in a low-ceilinged room, just under the state apartments, The Baby was being born. It was a pleasant room, looking onto a charming garden and over a shining stretch of water called the Round Pond; but that night it was a crowded room, as was its antechamber. It is the rule that witnesses must be present at the birth of royal children—just to be sure no one substitutes another baby if the child dies—and Edward was obeying every rule. His younger brother, the Duke of Sussex, was there, and the Archbishop of Canterbury. But the most important witness was England's great hero, the Duke of Wellington, who had defeated Napoleon at Waterloo.

At four-fifteen the Duke of Kent came out of the bedroom and into the antechamber and announced the birth of his daughter. He turned to Sir Frederick Wetherall, his faithful friend and equerry. "Please send for your little daughter Augusta," he said. "I would like her to be here."

The excited child arrived and the Duke entered the room again, this time carrying a tiny bundle. He held it out to Augusta, saying, "Take your Princess in your arms and be as loyal to her as your father has been loyal to me."

It was, as Victoria's father hoped, the beginning of a friendship between the girls that lasted all their lives. In fact, Augusta and a cousin of hers were among the few playmates the Princess had; there was half-sister Feodore, of course, but she was about ten years older than the Princess.

Victoria was a good, healthy baby and it was lucky she was, for the life of a royal infant was not all sleeping and eating and lullabies. On June 24, just four weeks from the day she was born, came the great christening. It was held in the beautiful "Cube" room at Kensington Palace, a room about as high as it is long and wide. It was, and still is, a most elaborate chamber, full of gilt statues and marble doorways and pillars. The ceiling is domed and, like the walls, is painted blue and gold. On this famous occasion, a royal gold christening font was brought from the Tower of London, and a crimson velvet covering for it was borrowed from the Chapel Royal in St. James's Palace.

The Archbishop of Canterbury, assisted by the Bishop of London, performed the ceremony, and the room was full of royal relatives. The Prince Regent was there, although the Kents were not expecting him, and he proceeded to make things difficult. The truth was that Edward wanted to call his daughter Elizabeth, after England's first great queen, but George had other ideas. When the Archbishop asked for the baby's name he said quickly, "Alexandrina."

Edward frowned. "There should be an additional name," he suggested.

"Certainly," agreed the Regent. "Georgina?"

"Or," countered the Duke of Kent, "Elizabeth?"

There was an uneasy silence and the tension in the room grew so obvious that Victoire burst into tears. "Very well," said the Prince Regent finally, "call her after her mother. But Alexandrina must come first."

Without consulting the baby's parents George had decided that, for political reasons, the Emperor Alexander of Russia must be one of the godfathers. So the Archbishop performed the ceremony and the bundle of lace and muslin became Alexandrina Victoria, which for the first few years of Victoria's life was shortened to "Drina." As she grew a little older, the diminutive was dropped and she became Victoria.

Victoria's second ordeal came when she was six years old, for she was the first royal baby to be vaccinated. From that time on, doctors all over the country could point to this important infant as a shining example, and persuade more timid parents that the new medical discovery was a valuable, even a necessary, safeguard.

These were extremely happy days for the Duke and Duchess of Kent; for they were devoted to their "little May Blossom," as the Duke affectionately called her. Like most fond fathers he boasted about his baby to anyone who would listen and showed her off on every possible occasion, even taking her to a military review when she was only four months old.

"Prinny," the Prince Regent, was disgusted with his brother. "That infant," he said sharply, "is too young to be brought into public!"

He was right; Victoria was much too young for such displays. But it did her no harm because she was a very strong baby—so strong that when the Bishop of London played the old game of tossing her up and catching her she pulled off his wig and then tore out a handful of his hair!

When the days began to grow longer and colder the Duke decided to move his little family to the warmer seashore, and by December they were settled at Sidmouth. When the new year came in, Edward suddenly remembered another prophecy someone had made to him—that two members of the royal family would die in 1820. The King, old George III, was failing fast and would surely be one to go. The Duchess of York was seriously ill, too. And the fat, puffing, wheezing Prince Regent looked as if he might drop dead at any moment. "My brothers," said the Duke of Kent to a friend, "are not as strong as I am; I have lived a regular life. I shall outlive them all. The crown will come to me and my children."

But poor, optimistic Edward, who had been so careful of his health in big ways, allowed himself to be careless in one little, fatal way. He went for a walk one rainy day in January and came home with wet feet. Instead of changing his shoes and socks immediately, he insisted on playing with his "little May Blossom" for an hour or so first. He caught cold, which turned into pleurisy, and on the 11th of January he died. Six days later the old mad King died, too; the prophecy was fulfilled.

II

Victoria's Childhood

The death of the Duke of Kent left his Duchess heartbroken and bewildered, for their marriage of convenience, made simply and purely to provide an heir for the throne of England, had proved to be a happy one. Victoire's first marriage had been arranged for political reasons, too, and her husband was a man much older than she was. She had had to make the best of it and the best had not been very good. In this, her second marriage, the best had turned out to be very good indeed. She and Edward soon discovered that they were congenial companions with the same aims and ambitions in life and, before they had been married long, they loved each other almost as much as if theirs had been a love match in the beginning.

What should she do now? Her first impulse was to bundle up her seven-month-old baby and return to Germany, but she knew that her husband had felt Victoria should grow up in England and that he had resisted the Prince Regent's attempts to send them back to Amorbach after the baby's christening. Money was a problem again, too; she couldn't pay for the Duke's elaborate funeral, to say nothing of another expensive trip.

Fortunately for the Duchess, her brother Leopold had rushed to her side when he heard of Edward's serious illness. Leopold had expected to share the throne of England with his wife, the Princess Charlotte, and now that she was dead he determined to play a big part in the upbringing of his niece Victoria. "Edward was quite right," he said firmly. "Victoria must grow up in England." He was still living in England then himself, as he did not become King of the Belgians until 1831.

The new King, for the Prince Regent was now George IV, king in title as well as deed, gave his permission for the widow and baby to return to Kensington Palace. Leopold contributed the necessary funds, and the sad entourage wended its way to London. It was a bitterly cold winter and a grim trip for the poor Duchess of Kent as she rode, heavyhearted, in the uncomfortable, unheated carriage. She tried not to think of her problems, the mountain of debts, and the responsibility of raising a queen in a country still strange to her.

However, Victoire was naturally good-natured and jolly and she adored her infant. The sisters of the new King were kind and attentive to her, and her brother Leopold decided to add a good round sum to her yearly income. And so, as the months turned into years, the

Duchess put her sorrow behind her and let the shining dream of a daughter on the throne of England rule her life. The Duchess of Clarence lost a second child and Victoria's chances seemed to be growing stronger.

Meanwhile Victoria was changing from a fat chunk of a baby who looked exactly like her Grandfather George to an equally fat, waddling toddler. She played around the rooms and halls of Kensington Palace with her nurse Mrs. Brock, whom she called "Dear Boppy," and romped happily with her pretty half-sister. Feodore loved the child dearly and never tired of amusing her, often riding her around the gardens for hours in a little hand carriage.

At four Victoria learned her alphabet and at five she started her studies. Her first guide and teacher was a gentle, wise, lovable woman named Louise Lehzen, who had come from Germany with the Kents in the capacity of governess to Feodore. The "little May Blossom" was then a stormy child who indulged in tantrums and refused to do what she was told. However, whatever Lehzen's magic method of training was, by the time Mr. Davys came to take over her education Victoria had learned to behave herself. In fact, she became quite a model student.

"When you are naughty," scolded her mother one day, "you make both me and yourself very unhappy."

"No," corrected Victoria. "No, Mamma, not *me*, not *myself*, but you."

Although the Princess had very few playmates she

was never alone. There was someone with her every moment—Lehzen, of course, or her mother. She ate her breakfast at eight, sitting in her own small rosewood chair with her bread and milk and fruit set on a matching table right beside her mother's chair at the grownups' table. She had her simple dinner there at two o'clock while her mother had lunch; and when her mother was home for dinner, Victoria was beside her having a light supper.

The child's day was a busy one, with studies and play and walks and drives filling the hours, and she was quite ready at night to crawl into bed. She slept in her mother's room wherever they were, and at home her little French bed was set up beside her mother's larger one.

Kensington Palace, with its mellow rosy red brick walls, its beautiful quiet gardens set out in the days of William and Mary, and its Round Pond—such an ideal place for a child to sail a toy sailboat—was a lovely home in which to grow up. Victoria and her mother now lived in rooms on the second floor next to what had been the state rooms, where the kings and queens of England had their royal ceremonies and their formal parties when it was the royal residence. Now they held them at St. James's Palace, right in the heart of London.

The Kents had a large, airy bedroom with many casement windows and a charming fireplace. Victoria loved the pretty white wooden furniture, with its cane backs painted in patterns of green and white and its pillows of white Chinese silk embroidered all over with leaves.

The sitting room was more formal, with a gilded sofa and chairs upholstered in crimson. Victoria, who grew to prefer the overelaborate, overstuffed, overcarved furniture that came into vogue during her reign and that is still called "Victorian," did not realize that she was sitting on a perfect example of the best taste of the Regency period. It was the fashionable style of the day and illustrated the interest of the Prince Regent in classic Greek and Roman lines, combined with gilt and rich fabrics.

Her nursery and schoolroom was another airy, high-ceilinged room, very simply furnished, and there she worked busily away at her lessons or, on rainy days, exercised with a pair of dumbbells. The rainy days, and there were many of them, were long and dull. Victoria had so few playmates; the Princess Feodore was much older than her little sister, and Lady Jane Ellice and Augusta Wetherall, who had been carefully chosen to play with the royal child, came to Kensington Palace only occasionally.

"Come," Lehzen would say when there was nothing else to do, "let us finish dressing our latest doll." It was the kind governess's hobby to dress little dolls to represent particular ladies of the time and Victoria would get her needle and thimble and help her. The Princess loved dolls and had over a hundred of them. Each new one was entered by name in a book and the group was divided into three families.

When the weather was fair, there was plenty to keep Victoria busy and happy. The dogs would frisk around, asking to be taken for a walk; her delightful pony cart was always available for rides around the large palace grounds; and her beloved donkey, given her by the Duke of York, was in the stable waiting for her. As a matter of fact, the Princess thought her donkey such a wonderful animal that, when she was invited to visit King George, she wanted to ride to Windsor Castle on him. She felt that the greatest treat she could give the King of England was to introduce him to her donkey.

Rain or shine, there was always music, which was a source of joy to Victoria all her life. She practiced piano and voice regularly, and sang duets with her mother. One day the Duchess sent for a famous child harpist, thinking her daughter might learn something of value from talking to her. The mother threw up her hands in horror when she came in and found the girls busily discussing their dolls!

The schoolroom hours passed pleasantly as a rule because the Princess was industrious by nature and loved her teachers. As she studied alone, there is no way of knowing where she would have ranked in a class of children her age; but, from her papers and from the lists of her reading, it seems obvious that she was an apt student.

A few months after her first formal lessons started

with Mr. Davys, her mother took her to Ramsgate by the sea for a holiday. This is a letter the five-year-old girl wrote home to her teacher:

My Dear Sirs,

I do not forget my letters

nor will I forget you.

Victoria

Perhaps the reason she did not forget her letters was that Mr. Davys made a game of learning them. He would write words on bits of paper and place them around the room, then call one out and send Victoria to find it.

While the Princess was being led gently along the path of learning in her nursery, the nurseries of Victoria's older uncles remained empty and King George made an occasional effort to honor his tiny niece. When she was four he sent her a miniature of himself, set in diamonds, and when she and her mother called to thank him for this gift he invited them to stay to dinner. Three years later he asked Victoria, the Duchess of Kent, and Feodore to Windsor Castle for a few days, and did everything he could to make their stay a pleasant one.

Victoria never forgot that visit nor the disgust that rose in her when they arrived at Windsor and the bloated, rouged and powdered, horrible-looking old man said "Give me your little paw," as she curtsied to him, and then put down his painted face for her to kiss. But, even at seven, the Princess managed to hide her revulsion.

The three days at the huge stone castle, the principal residence of the royal family for eight hundred and fifty years—parts of it date back to the days of William the Conqueror—were filled with happy expeditions. The young visitors were driven to see the King's collection of gazelles and chamois, and picnics and fishing parties were planned for them on the royal barge. There were drives to Virginia Water, a lake surrounded by a pleasure ground full of Chinese pagodas, fishing temples, and pavilions, and it was on one such outing that they met the King driving his own tall phaeton. He stopped both carriages when he saw Victoria and said, "Pop her in."

The Princess was lifted up over the high wheel and squeezed in between George and her Aunt Mary, who was driving with her fat brother. The Duchess of Kent watched the equipage drive off with her heart in her mouth, even though she could see that Princess Mary was holding Victoria firmly around the waist. The King was an experienced "whip," as they called the dandies of the day who drove their own carriages, but the phaetons were tippy affairs and it was the style to drive them very fast. This was a particularly gay one and the little girl was so entranced with the scarlet and blue livery of the grooms and the beautifully paced, fast-stepping horses that she wasn't at all nervous and enjoyed every minute of it.

One evening Victoria was dressed in her best frock and taken to the Royal Lodge, where the King had his private quarters. After a little while George, instead of sending for his niece, sought her out himself and took her by the hand. "Now, Victoria," he said, "the band is in the next room and shall play any tune you please. What shall it be?"

"Oh, Uncle," answered the tactful seven-year-old, "I should like 'God Save the King.'"

When the time came to say goodbye the King asked his visitor what she had enjoyed most at Windsor. Out came Victoria's answer in her clear, small, birdlike voice, "The drive with you."

This was undoubtedly the most exciting visit she had; but Victoria spent many happy weeks from time to time at Claremont, her Uncle Leopold's beautiful country estate. It was peaceful and delightful at Claremont, and Victoria always insisted she would rather be there than home at Kensington Palace.

Leopold, whom Victoria loved more dearly as each year passed, was carrying out his plan to help in her education and to see that she was brought up as a future queen should be. He spent a great deal of time with his guest during these visits, talking with her as one person to another—never as uncle to niece. Victoria listened carefully to everything he said and always tried to follow his good advice to the letter. When he became King of Belgium and moved to his new country, he and his niece wrote each other very often. I must write to Uncle Leopold, was the little girl's first thought when anything good or bad happened.

Another source of delight was the time spent in Tunbridge Wells, a lovely resort city with health-giving mineral springs. The Duchess of Kent owned a beautiful home there called Calverley House. It sat high above the city and was surrounded by luxurious gardens. It was always a happy change for Victoria when her mother moved their household there for a few summer weeks, and she would run up and down the beautiful curving staircase admiring its ironwork spindles and the smooth walnut handrail that felt like satin under her small hand. A less protected child would have seen at a glance that that stair banister was ideal for sliding down—but not Victoria!

The nursery was not as comfortable as the one at Kensington Palace. It faced north, instead of looking over the gardens, and the Princess grew tired of the striped blue and buff wallpaper. She much preferred the hours spent playing in the long, elegant drawing room with its floor-length windows that opened onto the sunny gardens. There were seaside holidays, from time to time, but her "dear Tunbridge Wells" held a special place in Victoria's heart.

So passed the childhood of a queen-to-be: walks, rides, lessons, toys, pets, visits—and always, always, someone beside her. A mother, a governess, a lady-in-waiting, a tall footman in red livery, a king—she was never allowed to be alone. It was an odd, formal existence, with everything carefully planned. Victoria never knew what it meant to walk home from school with a friend, to play with the boy next door, or to go to the kitchen for something to eat between meals.

The English people were now beginning to take an interest in this small Princess who was growing up at Kensington. When she was born in 1819 the country was just settling down after the long, long wars with Napoleon. Those wars had impoverished England and many lean years followed them, but 1819 was a rich year in other ways. Lord Byron was writing *Don Juan;* Sir Walter Scott finished *Ivanhoe;* Keats had just published *Endymion;* and it was Shelley's best period, for he wrote both *Prometheus* and *The Cenci* at that time. And while these authors were busy with immortal poetry and prose, Sir Thomas Lawrence, one of the greatest of English painters, was finishing his finest series of historical portraits.

The British Isles were fairly peaceful at this time,

despite the fact that the people did not like, nor had they ever liked, the line of kings who were ruling them. George I had succeeded to the throne because of many deaths in the line of succession. His mother was English, but he had been born and brought up in Germany; he was stupid and immoral and never, although he sat on the throne of England, learned to speak English. George II was rather like his father, but he stayed out of politics and so managed to keep the crown. George III, who was king when Victoria was born, was actually insane for years; before he became mentally incapable of ruling, he produced his huge family and meddled in politics to such an extent that many people blame him for the American Revolution.

George IV, who was Regent for his mad father, was not popular either as Prince Regent or as king. But, much as he was disliked, he had three brothers, all younger than the Duke of Kent, Victoria's father, whom the British people hated even more. That is why they watched Victoria's progress with interest and hope; rather than see Ernest, Augustus, or Adolphus, the youngest princes, wear the crown, they might have overthrown the monarchy.

These unpopular kings had done nothing to improve the lot of their subjects. Taxes were high because of their extravagance and the high cost of winning the recent wars. Crime was widespread and punishment too severe. Working conditions were unbelievably bad and the average living conditions little better. However, it was the end of a difficult time and things were going to improve; the wheel of progress was turning. And, in the schoolroom at Kensington Palace, a little girl was learning to be "good."

III

The Heiress to the Throne

"What a lovely evening for a ball!" said Victoria, following her mother into their carriage on a balmy night in May, 1829. "I wonder if the Queen of Portugal is looking forward to it as much as I am." She straightened her gauzy white muslin skirt and patted the soft blue satin sash with an air of quiet satisfaction; for the Princess loved dancing, and this party, planned by the King in honor of the ten-year-old visiting Queen, was her first ball.

"Remember that she is a year younger than you and probably can't speak English very well. Do your best to make her feel at ease, Victoria. I don't approve of evening parties for children, but the King insisted—"

Victoria missed hearing the rest of her mother's sentence because their carriage drew up just then behind two carved and gilded vehicles and she was leaning out of the window to see them better. They all pulled up in the courtyard of St. James's Palace and out stepped several elaborately dressed and bejeweled Portuguese courtiers, who solicitously escorted inside a slender, dark-haired girl.

"Mamma," whispered Victoria, her eyes widening, "that must be the Queen. But she looks so grown up and so pretty!"

The Duchess of Kent said nothing. She was only too well aware that everyone at the ball would be comparing the small, immature English princess with the early-ripening foreign beauty.

King George IV, looking as grand as a fat man could in his blue uniform and sparkling decorations, greeted his little guests with pomp and ceremony. The band struck up a gay quadrille and the ball began, with the young people twirling merrily to the music.

When waltz time came around, Victoria and Maria of Portugal sat side by side on a pair of special chairs and did their best to become acquainted. The waltz was a comparatively new dance in England and had been popular in polite society only since 1816, but it was still considered too intimate a dance for young, unmarried royalty.

Soon the girls went back to take their places in a lively square dance and Victoria was in the middle of a complicated figure when she heard a commotion nearby. There, on the floor, was Maria, a heap of dark curls and white ruffles and ribbon. She had slipped on the polished surface and hurt her face. Well, thought Victoria as she watched the sobbing girl leave the ballroom, she's not so grown up after all. That was the end of the party for Maria, but the English princess, delighting the onlookers with her poise and grace, stayed till dawn.

This, Victoria's first ball, was King George's last, for he died less than a month later. Frederick, Duke of York, the next in succession, had died in 1827; so William, Duke of Clarence, became William IV and soon thereafter Victoria, by making up the table of succession herself, realized that she was next in line to wear the Crown of England.

Life now became busier and lessons harder and Victoria had to make her first public appearances. "You and I are going to Bath," announced the Duchess of Kent one day to her daughter. "They are naming their new public park the Royal Victoria Park and they want you to open it for them. We will stay at the York House hotel and we should be most comfortable."

When the royal party arrived at their destination, Victoria looked around their large square room with pleasure. They should, indeed, be comfortable here. She admired the ornate, inlaid wardrobe and the matching dressing table and mantelpiece. But how many full-length mirrors there were! She skipped around, delightedly, seeing her small figure reflected from all angles, every place she turned; the wardrobe door was mirrored, the dressing table had a long pier glass, and the mirror over the fireplace seemed to double the width of the room.

While her mother superintended the unpacking and

saw that their own linen was put on the big, beautiful Chippendale four-poster bed which she would share with her child, Victoria wandered to one of the long windows and looked up the steep streets with their pale golden stone buildings.

"Mama," she said, "come and see how lovely the houses are here. Rows and rows of them, all matching and some of them make a curve."

"That's called a crescent," answered the Duchess. "Bath has many of them, and squares and terraces and circles. People come here to bathe in the Roman baths, dear; it became a fashionable health resort back in the days of your Great-uncle George. We must manage time to drive around and see it all, because it is one of England's most beautiful cities."

The Princess enjoyed the visit extremely and was pleased to hear later that, because she had stayed there, the York House was renamed the Royal York House and that the room was to be kept just as it was, for posterity to see and admire.

This was not too happy a period for Victoria, however, because Feodore married a German Prince and went off to Germany to live. Now she had no one to play with and confide in, and she found that she was expected to take Feodore's place as her mother's constant companion. The little Princess had always been sensitive to any tension around her, and the Duchess made no effort to conceal her dislike of the new King and her determination to quarrel with him whenever she could.

Victoria had to admit that her Uncle Billy was an odd-looking man, with his pineapple-shaped head, his popeyes, and his face reddened and rough from his years as a royal sailor. And the stories that reached Kensington Palace about his behavior made him sound peculiar, to say the least. The girl chuckled to herself as she thought of the description of his first few hours as king. It seems that as soon as William heard of his brother's death he rushed right up to St. James's Palace from his quiet home at Bushey Park. Instead of waiting for a royal carriage and a dignified escort, he tied a long crepe veil around his tall white hat, jumped into the handiest vehicle, and was off for town at full speed—bowing right and left to everyone he passed, with the crepe veil blowing wildly out behind him.

However, the queer, breezy monarch loved his tiny niece and made it clear that he expected his heiress to attend most of the Court functions. The first one was a chapter of the Order of the Garter, and Victoria enjoyed it very much. The Queen, her Aunt Adelaide, was a gentle, loving woman and she helped the little girl through all the formal ceremony. As they passed one group of bowing courtiers, Victoria heard a whisper—"She looks like an overdressed doll!"—and, when she caught a glimpse of herself in a long mirror, she thought perhaps it was true. There was something about the floor-length black veil and the wide-spreading Court train that made her seem even smaller than usual.

Later in the summer another invitation arrived. "Well,

Victoria," said the Duchess of Kent in an irritated voice, "here is a royal command to attend a Drawing Room in honor of your aunt's birthday. We will have to go."

By the time they reached the palace, the Duchess was in a bad temper and her daughter was so upset that she found it hard to concentrate on making her curtsies and saying the right, polite nothings to the right people. Oh, dear, she thought, what can Mother be saying to Uncle Billy? Her face is so red and her voice is so shrill! Surely they won't quarrel here in front of everyone. But I must not notice—I must not. Victoria was learning one of royalty's hardest lessons, to conceal her emotions in public.

The party ended and the exhausted child was glad to reach the sanctuary of her bed. She turned her head to the wall and pretended to be asleep when her mother came in.

In the peaceful days that followed, Victoria almost forgot the unhappy incident, not realizing that her mother was now annoying the King by being very difficult about their share in the plans for his coronation. So she was a bit surprised when the Kent household dashed off to the Isle of Wight not long before the date set for the Great Day. I hope we get back to London in time to have our robes fitted, she thought.

Victoria hurried home from the beach one day with a scraped knee. Her mother bandaged it carefully and then went to her desk. "I am writing your Uncle Billy that we cannot attend his coronation because you have injured your knee," she said. The Princess could not believe her ears! Not go to the coronation? Surely her mother was teasing her. "This will put William in his place," murmured the Duchess as her pen flew over the paper.

Poor Victoria! She burst into tears and fled to Lehzen for comfort. "Come play with your dolls," suggested that good lady. "No, no!" sobbed the Princess, facing her first great disappointment; it was one she would always remember.

Soon after this it was decided that Victoria should be examined by a board of educators to ascertain how she was progressing with her studies. It was an ordeal; but she passed it beautifully, to the delight of everyone concerned.

Victoria's thirteenth birthday rolled around and her Uncle Leopold, now King of the Belgians, wrote the Duchess of Kent that it was time the people of England had an opportunity to see something of their future queen. "Take her for a tour around the country and stay at some of the Great Houses," he suggested. The "Great Houses" are the ancestral homes of the oldest and wealthiest of the titled families.

"Leopold is right," decided Victoria's mother. So the plans were made, the trunks were packed, and the little Princess's bed was taken apart to travel with them. Just before they started, the Duchess handed her daughter a red leather book. "Here is a diary for you," she said, "and I want you to keep a faithful record of the trip in it. Put down what we do and see every day and I will read it to make sure you are keeping it properly."

Victoria murmured "Thank you," but her heart was not grateful. What good is a diary if someone else is going to read it? But she was obedient as usual, and as the carriages pulled away from the palace gates she wrote: "We left K.P. at 6 minutes past 7 . . . the road and scenery is beautiful. 20 minutes to 9. We have just changed horses at Barnet . . . 20 minutes past 10."

It was an exciting trip. Every place they went they were greeted by bands, speeches, welcoming committees, and each host and hostess tried to outdo the others in the lavishness of their hospitality. Even though the Princess became used to this, she was astonished when, on arriving at the home of a Lord and Lady Bulkeley at teatime, she saw that her hostess was dressed in white satin, blond lace, and orange blossoms, and that she was all asparkle with diamonds and peridots. "It's a ball gown, Mamma," she whispered.

Lady Bulkeley led them upstairs to her boudoir and Victoria stood transfixed. "Mamma!" she exclaimed. "Look at the beautiful dressing table, all draped in muslin and silk and lace. I've never seen anything so pretty." It was a new fashion even to the Duchess of Kent and she made a secret resolve as she watched her child's admiring face. She was glad Victoria could be so enthusiastic about anything after the weeks of gilded ballrooms, marble halls, picture galleries, formal gardens, dining tables loaded with gold dishes, and houses with so many rooms that they had to be guided around them.

November found the Princess home again and trying to settle down to the routine of the schoolroom. It wasn't too difficult because a group of stimulating new masters had been engaged to help with the artistic side of her education. Lablache, one of the most famous singers of the day, came to train her voice, and Taglioni, a great ballet dancer, was made responsible for her dancing and posture. Two well-known artists were hired to develop her skill with her drawing pencil. One was Sir Edwin Landseer, whose animal pictures will never be forgotten, and the other was Richard Westall, best known for his water colors of historical subjects.

By Christmastime, Victoria was glad to have another holiday and she waited for Christmas Eve and her presents with impatience. The evening arrived, dinner was finally over, and the drawing-room doors were thrown open. There stood two beautiful candlelit Christmas trees spreading their boughs over two tables loaded with gifts. And such gifts! An opal brooch and earrings, a pink satin dress, a fur-lined cloak, a silver brush, books—Victoria sighed as she admired the contents of the last package on her table.

"Now it is over for another year," she murmured.

"Perhaps not quite," answered her mother, and led the group to the door of the Princess's bedroom.

Victoria looked in and then stood very still. "Mamma," she said delightedly, "a dressing table just like Lady Bulkeley's!"

The holidays were soon over and the winter and spring that followed were so eventful that before Victoria knew it they were gone, too. She was going to operas and concerts now and reveling in the music. Her many lessons, her walks with her beloved spaniel Dash, and her rides on Rosy usually filled the days. If they weren't too full she fed and looked after her pets herself, which she loved to do.

The summer, her fourteenth, was the happiest so far, for the Kents went back to the Isle of Wight and had one of the royal yachts at their disposal. The Princess was a good sailor and felt right at home on the *Emerald*. And she had some young companions with whom to share all the pleasures—her cousins Prince Ernest and Prince Alexander of Württemberg. This was Victoria's first taste of the kind of fun that most girls take for granted and she was disconsolate when the morning arrived for the young men to start for home.

But it is hard to be gloomy when you are busy, and the Duchess had many things planned for the rest of the summer. There were trips on the *Emerald* to look forward to, and quite a few public ceremonies in which Victoria was expected to take the leading part. Unfortunately all was not smooth sailing, either on shipboard or on land.

The yacht ran into real danger one day with the Kents on board, and only the quick thinking of its captain kept them safe. Victoria, who never became panicky, looked immediately to see if Dash was all right. Yes, there he was under an officer's arm, and there he stayed until the emergency was over. It was always "animals first" with the Princess; later that year when one of her carriage horses fell down, her first thought again was for Dash. She snatched him out of the rocking vehicle and then turned to help her mother to safety.

The storm ashore was of the Duchess's making. Victoria wore her hair up now, and her poise and delightful manners aroused so much admiration that her mother became jealous and insisted on opening a pier at Southampton herself instead of allowing the little Princess to do it. The mayor and the townspeople were naturally disappointed and annoyed, and Victoria watched the unpleasant scene with a familiar feeling of shame and discomfort, keeping her round young face as expressionless as a block of wood.

King Leopold was aware, too, that Victoria was growing up and his letters were a source of delight and comfort. They were full of help and good advice to the young queen-to-be—and sometimes of praise. When she wrote him saying "You have sent to show me what a Queen *ought not* to be . . . send me what a *Queen ought to be,*" Leopold answered that she had written him a very clever, sharp little letter.

On the morning of July the 30th of her sixteenth summer, the Princess woke up early. She was in a serious, thoughtful mood because this was the day of her confirmation. As she put on the white lace dress and pinned up her hair with unusual care, her mind was busy. "I must become a true Christian," she resolved. "I must try to comfort dear Mamma in all her griefs, trials and anxieties and become a dutiful and affectionate daughter to her. I am truly sorry for all I have ever done that was wrong." She sighed, frowned at herself in the mirror, settled the white crepe bonnet with its white roses firmly on her head, and joined her waiting mother.

The royal family gathered in the chapel of St. James's Palace and Victoria sat nervously through the usual morning service. The King rose and took her by the hand and led her to the altar rail, followed by the Queen and the Duchess of Kent, and the rest of the group were directed to pews on each side of the altar. The tiny Princess was shaking a little, but she looked first at her Uncle William on one side and then at her mother on the other and took heart. She removed her bonnet and knelt before the Archbishop of Canterbury.

When it was over, the party proceeded to a small room called the Closet and the King and Queen handed her two velvet boxes. Victoria opened the first one and gasped; there, sparkling up at her, was a beautiful set of emerald jewelry. "Now open mine," said Queen Adelaide, smiling fondly at her. The second box lid popped up and disclosed a matching emerald tiara, nestling in the satin padding. "Oh," breathed the girl. "Oh! How beautiful! And," she added happily, "how grown-up!"

In less than two years the heiress to the throne would come of age and now she entered more and more into adult activities. Her social life had become a whirl of balls, concerts, and theater parties. King Leopold came over with his lovely new bride and Victoria joined quite naturally in all the festivities connected with their visit. She was more at ease now with new acquaintances; and when her cousins Ferdinand and Augustus arrived to stay at Kensington Palace, she felt very much at home with the young princes from Germany and they had a great deal of silly, gay fun together.

But the guests who made the deepest impression on Victoria were another pair of German princes—Ernest and his younger brother Albert of Saxe-Coburg-Gotha, a group of three duchies now, in 1837, united under the rule of Duke Ernest, the boys' father. They were expected at Kensington Palace a few days before her seventeenth birthday and the little Princess waited for word of their arrival wtih mixed emotions. It was an open secret that the Duchess of Kent's family had planned a marriage between Victoria and Albert from the time they were infants, and King Leopold, knowing that the young couple were to meet, had had a serious talk with his niece about the possibility.

Victoria wandered nervously around her room. She picked up a book and put it down. She practiced on the piano for a few minutes and stopped. Her mother looked in. "Come, Victoria, our guests have arrived," she said. Down they went to the elaborate state drawing room where, in the midst of all the gold and damask and statues and paintings, three men and one bird were waiting.

The Duchess kissed the men fondly and presented them to her child. Ernest was, Victoria thought, not very good-looking, but he had a kind, honest, intelligent expression. Her Uncle Ernest, the boys' father and her mother's brother, won her heart immediately with the warmth of his greeting and by presenting her with the enchanting bird perched on his finger. It was a tame lory, a strange genus of parrot.

And Albert? The two young people who were to go down in history as great lovers looked at each other for the first time. Oh, thought the Princess, how handsome he is! What large blue eyes, what a beautiful nose—I believe his hair is about the color of mine. And how I like his expression, so good and sweet and yet so clever and intelligent! She dropped her eyes demurely; no one but her diary and perhaps her Uncle Leopold must know how much she admired this young man at first sight.

The first shyness between the three cousins soon wore off and they enjoyed themselves to the utmost. The days sped by as they walked and rode together, attended operas and concerts, played and sang just for their own amusement, romped around Kensington Palace almost like ordinary playmates, and laughed delightedly at one another's jokes. Albert, who hated evening parties and always got sleepy at them, was especially witty at breakfast. He was the ringleader in most of the fun and had a way of playing with Dash that always made Victoria giggle.

The high point of the visit was Victoria's birthday ball. As the Princess danced the enchanted hours away, she knew that it was an evening she would always remember. Too soon it was three-thirty and she and Albert were dancing a last country dance together. She sighed as the music stopped—a perfect ball and a perfect partner.

On her cousins' last morning Victoria came down to breakfast with a mournful face. "Come," said Albert, "this must be another happy meal together." She did her best, but it was a wet-eyed girl who watched their carriage out of sight.

A short time before the Coburgs' visit the Duchess of Kent had added seventeen rooms to her suite at Kensington Palace. The Princess, reveling in the added comfort of their charming and airy new quarters, did not know that the King had refused her mother permission to occupy more rooms and that she had simply taken them without his knowledge.

Victoria realized that her mother's dream of ruling England as Regent was fading with each passing year. And she knew that underlying all the quarrels with William was her secret wish that he would die before Victoria came of age, so that she would be Regent for her daughter. The King tried to be patient with her, but it grew increasingly difficult. After the Coburgs left he invited her and Victoria to Windsor for a triple celebration, as he and Adelaide and the Duchess of Kent all had birthdays within a few days of one another in

August. The Duchess coolly replied that they would arrive in time for William's birthday, making no apology for missing the Queen's or for not sharing hers with them.

This apparently was the last straw—plus the fact that news of the Kents' new quarters had reached his ears. So, early on the day they were to arrive at Windsor Castle, he made a quiet trip to Kensington Palace to see what the Duchess had been up to. He saw! That evening he strode into the elaborate drawing room at Windsor, welcomed Victoria affectionately, and then turned to her mother.

"You have taken an unwarrantable liberty," he said in an embarrassingly loud and carrying voice. "Not only without my consent, but against my express command." As he went on berating the Duchess for her disrespectful conduct, the assembled company was glad to slip away. All but poor Victoria. Her shamed heart sank as she climbed the stairs. It was going to be an ordeal to share a room with her mother that night!

The next evening was the big birthday banquet. Victoria sat opposite King William, and the Duchess of Kent was on his right. He rose to answer the toast to his health; suddenly his face flushed angrily and his voice grew loud and uncontrolled. "My one hope and prayer," he roared, "is that I shall live nine months longer . . . so there will be no danger of the Regency of a person now near me, who is surrounded by evil advisers and is herself incompetent to act with propriety in the station in which she would be placed. I have been grossly and continuously insulted by that person. That young lady"—looking at Victoria—"has been kept away from my Court. I am King. I shall insist and command that the Princess do upon all occasions appear at my Court, as it is her duty to do."

Queen Adelaide blushed. Victoria burst into tears. The Duchess of Kent sat quite still and silent, white with anger and mortification. The embarrassed guests, over a hundred in number, left the room without a word. Then the Duchess rose and demanded her carriage. "I shall not spend another night under this roof," she announced icily.

Gentle Adelaide stepped to her side and, by using every bit of tact she had, persuaded the Duchess to stay until morning. Victoria listened to them with a feeling of desperation, trying to control her tears. She knew she should not be showing any emotion, but she could not help it. It was the worst experience she had ever had in public. She did not realize it, but this was a turning point; there would be no more scenes between the King and her mother—indeed, her mother's rule over her was rapidly drawing to a close.

IV

A Very Young Queen

Victoria found it difficult to put King William's embarrassing "prayer" out of her mind. As the fall and winter passed and her eighteenth birthday came nearer and nearer, it was natural for her to look forward and wonder what coming of age would mean to her. Any thought of that important day was followed by the memory of her uncle's words: "My one hope and prayer is that I shall live nine months longer."

His prayer was answered. William lived to see his niece's eighteenth birthday and to know that the Duchess of Kent would never be Regent. But, when May rolled around and Victoria's big day was only a few weeks off, the King fell ill and it looked as if he would not live until the twenty-fourth after all. His condition was the result of several serious ailments and he weakened visibly from day to day. But his illness had its ups and downs and he showed an encouraging improvement just before the birthday.

Ill as he was, he managed to irritate the Duchess of Kent by sending Victoria a letter offering her an allowance of ten thousand pounds a year for her own use, and by insisting that his letter be presented to her personally. For a few minutes Victoria listened to her mother's furious reaction, then went quietly to her desk and wrote her uncle a loving letter of grateful acceptance.

She put her pen down and pressed her hand to her forehead. How her head ached! Would her mother never stop talking in that angry voice? It seemed to go round and round in the girl's head and mingle with the pain.

The day before the birthday another message came from Windsor saying that the King was better and wanted his niece's Coming of Age Ball to be held even though neither he nor his queen could be present. Victoria went to bed early that night in anticipation of the exciting day ahead.

The silky brown head stirred on its pillow. Something had wakened her. Could it be music that early in the morning? Yes, it was! Victoria was wide-awake now and she jumped out of bed and rushed to the window. The garden was full of singers, serenading her. What a wonderful way to be awakened on your eighteenth birthday, she thought.

This was indeed Victoria's day, and golden hour followed golden hour with nothing to spoil it. The whole of England made a holiday of it, and every place she went there were flags and decorations in her honor; even the coach horses wore lilac blossoms and May buds.

Very happily she dressed for the ball that evening and took a final look in the mirror before going downstairs. The face that smiled back at her was not a dazzlingly pretty one but it was young and sweet and charming, and the white ballgown set off her softly rounded figure to perfection. The off-the-shoulder neckline was a becoming frame for her white shoulders, and she was conscious of the fact that her flowers and long gloves and little slippers were in perfect taste.

As the Kent carriage drove from Kensington Palace to St. James's Palace, the streets were lined with a cheering throng eager to see their Princess. Victoria turned to her mother with tears in her eyes. "I feel very touched," she said, "that they should be so anxious to see poor, stupid me." The crowd grew and they found the palace courtyard jammed with spectators. So it was an excited girl who stood up with young Lord Fitzalan for the first dance, and continued on through the enchanted evening with princes and marquises and earls as her partners.

The news from Windsor was not so cheerful the next day and it was now apparent that the King's improvement had been only temporary. Word went to Leopold in Belgium that the end was imminent and he sent his trusted adviser, Baron Stockmar, to England to guide his niece through the coming important and difficult time.

By the middle of June the bulletins on William's condition were so grave that all social activities at Court were canceled. The little household at Kensington Palace received no visitors and Victoria's lessons were stopped. She spent a great deal of her time conferring with Baron Stockmar, preparing herself for the crucial hours ahead.

The girl's thoughts were often with her dying uncle during these sad days and she remembered with affection all his many kindnesses to her. "Poor man," she said to herself, "he was odd and singular but his intentions were often ill-interpreted. He meant well, I know." William's tiffs with her mother had not prejudiced Victoria against him and she waited for the news of his death with a heavy heart.

They were emotionally wearing days for the Princess. Her notes to Leopold and her journal were full of her knowledge of the seriousness of her position and of her determination to carry out her part with honor and grace. She studied her Uncle Leopold's letters and decided to follow his good advice in every way. "Begin by taking everything as the King leaves it," he said, "this way you gain time. Keep your mind cool and easy. . . . Stick firmly to your resolution when once taken. Be courageous, firm and honest. It is excessively difficult to retrace a false move to get out of a mistake, so act most cautiously."

Leopold had, as a matter of fact, thought of coming to his niece's side during this time. He finally decided to come later, instead. People, he felt, might misinterpret his motives and think he was trying to be a power behind the throne.

The shadowy, anxious period was ending at last. It was bedtime at Windsor Castle on the night of June the nineteenth, but the huge, sprawling building was a hive of lights and unhappy activity. Kings and queens cannot be born or live or die in privacy, and William IV's blundering, well-meaning life was drawing to a close. Midnight. One o'clock. Two o'clock. The King's breathing slowed . . . stopped. The King was dead. Long live the Queen!

A short time later a carriage drew up to one of the castle's great heavy doors and into it stepped the Archbishop of Canterbury; Lord Conyngham; and Victoria's doctor, Sir Henry Halford. Off they went, the horses' hoofs ringing out on the cobblestones of the huge courtyard. They bowled swiftly over the deserted roads between Windsor and Kensington Palace, their route taking them for miles beside the quiet, dark river Thames. Soon they reached the spreading huddle of buildings that was London and the trip was almost over.

It was five o'clock now and the first signs of dawn were in the summer sky. The gray horses pulled up at the gates of Kensington Palace, which was lighted by flickering lamps. One of the coachmen tugged hard on the bell. The porter's lodge by the left gate showed no sign of life, so he rang the bell louder. The other coachman joined him and they knocked and hallooed. Finally a sleepy, cross porter emerged, buttoning a coat over his nightshirt.

"What is the meaning of all this noise?" he demanded. "It is much too early to let anyone into the palace. Go away!"

Lord Conyngham stuck his head out of the carriage window. "Open up, man, open up! We are here on important business and you have kept us waiting much too long already."

"It is too early for business," protested the porter. "Come back later."

Lord Conyngham's voice grew stern. "Open up, you fool. We have come to see *The Queen.*"

These magic words opened the gate, and the carriage proceeded to the palace doors. Here all was dark and locked, too, and there was another delay before another sleepy porter came out. He, however, realized at once what had happened. He ushered the committee into the comptroller's parlor and hurried Victoria's maid to them so fast that she rushed downstairs in just a petticoat and mantle.

"We must see your mistress immediately," said the Archbishop. The girl disappeared and soon ran back into the room. "Oh, sirs," she wailed, "the Princess is sleeping so sweet I haven't the heart to wake her!" The men exchanged impatient glances and sent her up again. This time she called the Duchess of Kent and the Baroness Lehzen. The Duchess came down immediately to see whether she could not take charge of the situation herself.

"Madam," was the answer from the tired waiting men, "we must see the Queen. Now."

Victoria wakened out of a deep sleep and saw her mother standing by the side of the little French bed.

"Come, dear," she said, looking anxiously into her daughter's face, "the Archbishop of Canterbury and Lord Conyngham are waiting to see you."

"Oh," said Victoria, understanding what she meant.

She caught up a loose white cotton robe, tossed her hair back on her shoulders, picked up the silver candlestick from her bedside table, and was ready to start downstairs. Lehzen, carrying a bottle of sal volatile in case her nursling should feel faint, followed her through the door, which is now famous for its part in this historic moment, and the three women made their way to the room where the Queen was awaited.

The Duchess took a tentative step forward, holding her daughter's hand. But Victoria, for the first time in her life, freed herself and, leaving her mother's side, entered alone. The small, slight, girlish figure advanced into the room, her long light hair shining in the rays of the upheld candle. She stood, straight and silent, before the three men: the Archbishop, in all his clerical dignity; Lord Conyngham, representing the State; and, standing quietly by in case he should be needed, her own familiar doctor.

"Your uncle died tonight at twelve minutes past two,"

said Lord Conyngham, "and so you are now Queen." He stepped forward and, dropping to his knees, delivered the official announcement of the King's demise.

Victoria held out her hand for its first kiss of homage. Lord Conyngham was surprised at her doing this so easily and automatically. But he need not have been—the young Queen was just carrying out her part in a scene she had played in her mind for many years.

The Archbishop now saluted his new monarch. "Queen Adelaide suggested that I accompany Lord Conyngham," he said, "as she wanted me to tell you about the King's last moments. He was in a perfectly happy, quiet state of mind and was quite prepared for his death. His sufferings were not great."

Victoria thanked him for the comfort of his words, charged Lord Conyngham with messages of condolence and sorrow for her aunt, and left the room.

It has been said that she then broke down and cried on her mother's shoulder. If she did, it was the last time for many a year. She went up to her room immediately and donned a dark dress, out of respect for the late King. Henceforth she was no longer Princess Victoria, daughter of the Duchess of Kent. She was Queen Victoria and the Duchess was the Queen's mother, subject to her daughter's wishes and commands.

The rest of the morning was a busy one. Baron Stockmar conferred with the girl while she breakfasted, and then she hurried to her desk to write the news to Feodore and her Uncle Leopold. Those two notes were the first that she signed Victoria R.—Victoria Regina. The first letter she received addressed to her as queen was the one that had arrived early that morning from Lord Melbourne, asking permission to call on her at nine o'clock.

"I shall see him alone, Mother," announced the girl after she read it. "I shall always see my ministers alone."

A carriage drove up to the palace door just as the clock struck nine and out stepped Lord Melbourne, the Prime Minister and head of the Whig party. He was a good-looking man and, as he was in full ceremonial dress, he was a stunning figure as he strode in and asked to see "The Queen." The dark blue tail coat with its rich gold braid, the white breeches and the white silk stockings, the ostrich-feather-edged cocked hat, the sword and the gloves—everything about this costume which the Prime Minister wore on state occasions added importance and dignity to the man and the moment. He was shown up to Victoria's sitting room, where she awaited him.

Holding out her small hand for his kiss of homage, she said, "Lord Melbourne, it has long been my intention to retain you and the rest of the present Ministry at the head of affairs. I know that it could not be in better hands than yours." Her voice was clear and sweet and she smiled warmly at him after she finished her little speech.

The Prime Minister, moved by his new Queen's friendliness and by the emotion of the occasion, kissed her hand again. A long, close, rewarding companionship began at that moment.

Business came next and Melbourne read Victoria the declaration he had written for her to deliver that morning at her first council meeting.

"It is a very fine one," she said when he had finished.

They talked a bit more and then Lord Melbourne took his leave, telling his Queen he would see her again for a short conference at eleven, before the council convened.

Victoria went back to her desk and wrote her Aunt Adelaide a loving note of condolence, tactfully addressing it to the Queen of England.

The lady-in-waiting to whom she handed it said, rather timidly, "You know, Your Majesty, that Queen Adelaide is now the Queen Dowager."

"I realize that," answered Victoria, "but I shall not be the first to remind her of it."

It was now nearly eleven and Victoria made ready for the ordeal ahead of her. She knew that this first ceremony was an important one and that all the officers of state would be curious to see how she handled herself. She decided to wear a simple dark morning frock and no jewelry or adornment of any kind.

She was all ready when Lord Melbourne, who had been conferring with Mr. Greville, the Clerk of the Council, came in to tell her how the meeting would proceed. "The King's death will be announced formally to the assembled Lords," he said, "while you wait in the adjoining room. Then a few of us will come to you to make the same announcement. Mr. Greville wants to know if you want some of the officers of the state to accompany you when you enter the council chamber to read your speech."

Victoria thought for a minute. "No," she answered firmly, "I shall come in alone."

The ceremony went as planned and the great moment came when the doors were thrown open and the young girl, walking gracefully and easily, came in and faced the assembly of men. She bowed, took her seat at the head of the table, and read her speech in a clear, distinct, and completely audible voice. After she had finished, showing no nervousness or embarrassment whatever, she took and signed the oath for the security of the Church of England.

The Privy Councilors next swore their allegiance to their new monarch, kneeling and kissing her hand. Victoria was prepared for this, but she could not help blushing a little when she saw that the two royal dukes, her elderly uncles, were first. She kissed them warmly, getting up from her chair and moving over to the Duke of Sussex. He is too old to kneel, she thought. I am really just their young niece. How odd this all is!

The rest of the Lords came one by one and the Queen received their homage with graceful modesty and self-possession. As Mr. Greville said afterward, she showed no consciousness of the difference in rank between individuals. She looked to Lord Melbourne from time to time for guidance and, when the ceremony was over, retired from the room with the same dignity with which she had entered.

The assembled Lords broke up into little excited groups when the doors closed behind the girl. The room buzzed with praise and admiration for her manner and behavior. As Victoria had been so closely guarded by her mother and her governess, no one at Court had had an opportunity to talk to her alone; no one knew her, really, or could have ventured a guess as to how she would conduct herself in public. Sir Robert Peel, later to be one of England's Prime Ministers, turned to Mr. Greville and said, "I am amazed at her firmness, at her apparent deep sense of her situation. She seemed awed but not daunted."

The Duke of Wellington joined in. "If she had been my own daughter," he said, "I could not have desired to see her perform her part better."

The Duchess of Kent had waited outside the council rooms for her child. "Well, Victoria," she said as the girl joined her, "I need not ask you how you acquitted yourself, for you are quite composed. Were you not startled at finding yourself in a room alone with so many gentlemen?"

"No," answered Victoria quietly. "It was my duty to face them and God gave me all the strength I needed." She paused a moment. "I suppose, Mamma, it must be true that I am Queen of England?"

"Yes, love, you see that you are."

"Well, then, I have a request to make," said the Queen of England, who had never had a room to herself or even been allowed to walk downstairs alone. "I want to be alone and undisturbed for an hour."

The Duchess turned white and walked out of the room. Victoria, reveling in the luxury of solitude, sent out a series of royal orders that almost broke her mother's heart. "I shall have my dinner *alone*, and I want my bed moved to a bedroom of my own." The Queen's mother knew now that somehow, through the years, she had lost her child. As she had missed her opportunity to reign as Regent, so she must now give up hope of sharing her daughter's throne as beloved Mother Adviser.

Victoria retired to her room that night and, tired as she was, finished an account of the day's happenings in her journal. Then, in wonderful privacy, she undressed and put what had been that day a very queenly head, indeed, on the pillow and fell asleep.

V

Victoria Is Crowned

Victoria surrendered her opera cloak to the man waiting for it and stepped forward, looking down on the sea of faces turned up toward her. Covent Garden Theater was filled to capacity on this particular evening in November, 1837. Byron's tragedy *Werner* was popular with London theater-goers, but the real reason for their presence was that their new little Queen would, for the first time since her accession, occupy the elaborately draped royal box.

The excited audience gave her ovation after ovation and Victoria's heart swelled with happy gratitude. She steadied the dainty posy she held in her hands and hoped that the small tiara on her smooth bands of hair was still straight. She knew her soft, low-necked gown with its matching redingote bordered with swansdown was becoming; she had chosen it carefully for this public appearance.

The Duchess of Kent, standing slightly behind her

royal daughter, was draped in heavy-looking black lace and, as usual, wore a huge hat loaded with ostrich feathers. The audience resumed their seats and chattered admiringly, but not about the Duchess in her fancy toilette. It was all the Queen, the Queen, the Queen—what dignity, what charm, what presence! Yes, they all agreed, she was every small inch a queen.

The evening passed. The curtain fell. The audience sang "God Save the Queen" with unusual fervor and Victoria stepped back in the box to put on her cloak. As she and her party descended the stairs and left by the special door, they did not know that within the next few minutes a serious panic was narrowly averted in Covent Garden. The management had allowed too many standees that night and they jammed the aisles, making it impossible for people to get out of their seats. Fortunately, before anyone was hurt, someone in the dress circle leaned down and lifted a trapped spectator out by the elbows. Others followed suit and the scare was soon over.

The young Queen, riding home quietly in the royal carriage, sighed with weariness. It had been a busy few months since her Uncle Billy's death. For one thing, she and her mother had moved from Kensington Palace to Buckingham Palace. It was hard to leave the old home, but Victoria decided herself that Buckingham should be her London residence. George III had bought it many years before as a possible home for his wife in the event of his death. George IV thought it would be a splendid royal residence and spent a great deal of money having it remodeled. The work went on into William's reign, but he decided not to use it.

Life in the new home was not very comfortable for Victoria that summer, because the great rooms and halls still swarmed with workmen painting, plastering, altering partitions and stairways. And, although no one ever mentioned it, the drains were faulty. Indoor bathrooms were an innovation still and sanitation was an only partly solved problem. However, the gardens were lovely and Dash adjusted himself very well. He and his little mistress spent many happy hours romping in the secluded greenery, where they could be simply a girl and her dog.

After the move Victoria settled down to learning her job. The British empire at this time was vast and widespread, including the British Isles (England, Scotland, Ireland), the British West Indies, the Bahamas, Canada, British Guiana, Gibraltar, Malta, Ceylon; there were British settlements in Africa and Australia, and part of India was under British rule.

Naturally there was a great deal to learn about this empire. But the young Queen knew much of her lesson already. She was quite familiar, for instance, with the constitution of her government and how it worked. She knew that her country was ruled by Parliament, which consists of the House of Commons and the House of Lords. The members of the House of Commons are elected by the people, and the seats in the House of Lords are held mostly by hereditary right. The duties and privileges of the Houses are divided and different, but the House of Commons is the more powerful and important group and carries the burden of government.

At this time, general elections for seats in the House of Commons were held every seven years—instead of every five years, as now. However, the government could be, and can still be, dissolved at any time by a Parliamentary defeat of the party in power. In other words, if a measure proposed by the Cabinet is voted down by the House, it is a signal for the resignation of the Cabinet and the forming of a new one by the opposition party. In actual practice, at this time, a new government was formed about every three or four years; occasionally there would be a change in power after just a few months of new leadership.

There were two political parties, the Whigs and the Tories. Soon after Victoria came to the throne they became known by names that show the difference between them. The Whigs became the Liberals, and the Tories the Conservatives.

When the party in power suffers a defeat, the Prime Minister, who is the leader of the party, hands his resignation to his monarch. The Queen (or King) then summons the leader of the opposition party and asks him to form a new government. This means that she is appointing him Prime Minister and that he must choose a new cabinet.

Victoria knew that it was also her special duty or prerogative to summon new Parliaments, to open and close their sessions with a speech, to adjourn and dissolve the House of Commons, and to assent to bills passed by both Houses. In theory it was her privilege to veto bills thus passed, but in practice the royal veto had not been used since 1707. However, she did not want to be, nor was she, just a figurehead, and she insisted on having all important government decisions brought to her attention for her opinion and approval.

The young Queen realized only too well how much she had to learn about foreign and domestic affairs; but her formidable task was not unpleasant, for Lord Melbourne was the kindest and dearest of teachers and his little pupil turned to him as naturally as a flower turns to the sun. "Dear Lord Melbourne," she said to him one day, "I really enjoy our meetings and paper work. I like to be busy, you know. And you must always sit beside me at dinner so that we can talk over the events of the day."

The handsome Prime Minister looked fondly down on his Queen. He, too, enjoyed their working hours together. He thought back over his many years as a statesman and realized that they had somehow been rather empty. This eager, appreciative pupil of his was filling a void in his heart. He smiled. It was like having a daughter to love and guide.

The Court often smiled, too, as they watched them together. They said that the teacher-pupil relationship was working two ways—that, while Lord Melbourne was teaching Victoria how to be Queen, Victoria was teaching him better manners. He was witty, charming, and well-bred, but he had always been careless in his speech, manners, and appearance. Without saying very much, the Queen changed all this. Melbourne no longer sprawled in his chair, spoke without considering his audience, or lingered over his wine while the ladies waited for him in the drawing room. He looked and acted very much the Prime Minister now, and he was careful to follow the pattern of social small talk that Victoria preferred.

The meetings and paper work were only part of the Queen's new tasks. There were ceremonies in which she had to take part, speeches to be read, heavy robes to wear, and always people to greet. The Emperor of Russia sent her the diamond-studded decoration of the Order of St. Catherine, and after its presentation she held her first large reception. She wrote in her diary that night that it had all gone very well and that, by her own count, her hand had been kissed nearly three thousand times!

The guests thought the reception went very badly. The pages were new and rushed the ladies through the line so fast that many never got to see the Queen at all. They were all dressed in deep mourning, with long black veils and great black plumes, so that it was difficult for friends to find one another in the overcrowded rooms.

Soon it was summer and one rainy day in August the royal household packed its trunks and moved to Windsor. Victoria rode along through the damp countryside with a heavy heart and eyes as wet as the carriage windows. Oh, dear, she thought, how can I bear to sit on poor Uncle Billy's throne and in his chair at the table? And I know they will put me in Aunt Adelaide's rooms, where she was so unhappy!

The royal entourage rolled into the main street of Windsor and, despite the weather, it was lined with cheering townsfolk. This warm welcome dried the young Queen's tears and soon a happy, bright face smiled right and left at her people.

It was a wonderful summer. There was work to do, of course, but the horses were brought around every fair day and the countryside soon became accustomed to seeing Victoria gallop by dressed in a simple dark green riding habit and plain black beaver hat, surrounded by her ladies and gentlemen.

Guests came and went and Victoria had the great delight of entertaining her Uncle Leopold and his lovely queen. As a matter of fact she enjoyed the visit more than her uncle did, because he saw that he was no longer her chief councilor. One man would always stand first with the Queen, and Lord Melbourne now had that honor.

November came and it was time to move back to London. Victoria sat at her desk and wrote in her little leather book—"the pleasantest summer I EVER passed in *my life.*" Her pen slowed as she remembered all the happy weeks. There was the wonderful day when she first reviewed her troops. How exciting it was to dress in the stunning red and blue military habit and ride smartly up to the soldiers and answer their crisp salutes with one of her own! I really felt like a man, she mused. I believe I could fight at the head of my troops.

Life had been peaceful at Windsor Castle, but it was stimulating in London that fall and winter. The first big event of the season was a dinner for the Lord Mayor. Victoria woke up that morning with a bad headache and thought with dread of the hours ahead of her. She was out of mourning now and she knew she must wear her most elaborate dress—a pink satin one trimmed with gold and pearls. And she would have to put a heavy diamond diadem on her aching head. This was certainly one day, she decided, that she would like to be just plain Victoria Kent.

But the royal show must go on, and by the time she was seated in the great gold coach with its eight white horses her headache had gone. The streets were jammed with cheering subjects, and every window and balcony along the route to the Guildhall overflowed with spectators. When the coach arrived at its destination there were ceremonies and formalities to be lived through, and then the small Queen, followed by hundreds of excited guests, was ushered into the huge banquet hall. She gasped at the sight before her; the long narrow room, with its vaulted ceiling, its magnificent crystal chandeliers, and its columned walls, was a mass of stunning flags. The banquet tables were resplendent with miniatures of London's monuments and piles of brightly colored fruit, with sparkling glasses and beautiful china and silver.

She took her place at the table of honor thinking that she had never seen such a display of gowns, jewels, plumes, and uniforms. She felt rather dwarfed in the tall thronelike chair, and it was uncomfortable to eat while hundreds of eyes watched every bite. "I will grow accustomed to it," she told herself. "I will have to!"

As the winter came on she found that she did get used to being on display. Her people became used to seeing their Queen and she could attend the theater or opera without causing much excitement. She was extremely popular at this time and all the diaries and journals of the day were full of praise for her queenliness and charm. A bit later, when she had a short, giddy period of reveling in balls and parties, there would be a bit of criticism. In her own later years she deplored this time of innocent fun, harmless as it was.

The Court moved to Windsor after Christmas. It was deep in snow and, for the first time since 1814, the Thames was almost frozen over. Victoria and Lord Melbourne sat as close to the fire as they could when they met to talk over affairs of state. The new coal-burning grates didn't throw out as strong a heat as had the old log fires, but it was steadier. Victoria put on the warmest petticoats and stockings she could find, but the great rooms were chilly and drafty. The problem that she and the Prime Minister discussed most often was one of difficulties with the French Canadians up in cold Canada, and the atmosphere of Windsor Castle made it all seem very real to them.

Canada, which had belonged to the French until Wolfe took it for the British in 1760, was a divided country. The French and the English had not merged into one people, and their constitution, which called for a Governor and an Executive Council nominated by the government in England, a Legislative Council appointed for life in the same way, and a Representative Assembly elected for four years by each province, was working very badly. Grievances had festered and, before the proper reforms could be brought about, there was an insurrection in Lower Canada, the section populated mostly by French Canadians. Upper Canada had disturbances, too, and the Crown had to send troops to quell the uprisings. Now that there was real trouble, the problem of Canada was given serious consideration and, in 1840, Upper and Lower Canada were united and a system of colonial freedom was established by the English government.

When the snow was gone and the Court was back in Buckingham Palace, the big topic of conversation was Victoria's coronation. The Cabinet met in March and decided on June the twenty-eighth as a good date. Although actual preparations for the great ceremony had been under way for some time, there were the usual red tape and blundering; the result was that the workmen who had to turn out the decorations and ceremonial robes by hand found themselves with only seven weeks to complete everything.

Victoria was at her desk one day when she heard a tap at the door. She had been expecting it, so she put down her pen and greeted her visitor. He was a member of the Coronation Committee, followed by a page boy with a large box.

"Good afternoon, ma'am," he said. "May we bother you to try on the crown?"

The box was unlocked and the beautiful mass of gold and jewels with its cap of velvet and fur which had been worn by George IV and William IV was lifted out of its satin nest. Victoria sat obediently while it was settled on her small head. It came down over her ears and shifted heavily from side to side.

"It isn't very comfortable," she protested. "I'm afraid it will fall off if I stand up or try to walk with it on."

"Yes," was the answer, "it simply will not do. We'll have to reset the jewels in a smaller one designed to fit you."

That was just one of the problems that arose. She could not wear any of the robes used by her uncles and there had to be gowns to wear under her robes, and bags made to keep them in; this meant hours of fittings to be worked into the already busy schedule. There were invitation lists to approve and train bearers to choose.

King Leopold wrote Victoria in April that it might be wiser if he and Queen Louise did not attend, inferring that his niece should be the only queen present on her Day of Days. He expected Victoria to appreciate this polite gesture but to insist on their coming and he was a bit hurt when she wrote back accepting his decision not to come.

By the first of June, London was crowded with visitors. Whenever the tiny Queen ventured outside the tall metal gates of Buckingham Palace she found the streets jammed with sightseers. The Court chattered about the shortage of hotel accommodations for friends from out of town. Every boardinghouse was booked up and anyone who had a spare room to rent out reaped a happy harvest. Victoria and her committees had to house royal visitors and royal relatives from all over the world and to plan banquets and balls for their entertainment.

It was an unusually hot summer. While the visitors were amusing themselves with visits to Madame Tussaud's waxworks, watching balloon ascensions, driving out to Epsom for the races, hundreds of seamstresses were sewing night and day to finish the new costumes ordered by the ladies of fashion. Working conditions were unbelievably bad and the heat made them worse; many of the girls fainted at their tables as they stitched on the silk walking dresses, the elaborate evening gowns, the bonnets, shawls, pelisses, and parasols.

June waned and Coronation Day drew near. Victoria watched the decorations going up along the Mall, the wide avenue leading from the gates of the palace. She knew that stands would be built along every possible foot of the route taken by the royal procession—in front of clubs, shops, homes, public buildings. At night, as she stood and looked down, the decorations, which were merely pretty by day, were dazzling to see. The city seemed to be a fairyland of colored lights. Some were gaslights and some were oil, both rather dangerous kinds of outdoor illumination. I do hope we don't have any fires, she mused.

The Queen woke with a start as the great cannons announced that this was her day to be crowned. The bedside clock said four and she burrowed back under the covers. "I really should sleep a little longer," she told herself. "This is going to be such a long and tiring day." She managed to drowse a bit, but the increasing noise from outside kept waking her; the streets around the palace were filling rapidly with excited spectators and there were bursts of music from wandering bands. It was raining, but the weather did not seem to discourage the early birds.

Just before seven Victoria gave up and rang for her early tea. Then she climbed out of bed and began to dress slowly, wandering to the windows every few minutes to see the crowd below and to look hopefully for a break in the gray, clouded sky.

At nine-thirty the Queen, robed and ready, left her bedroom and joined a group of family and court ladies. At ten they descended the grand staircase and proceeded to the palace entrance, where the gold coach of state waited. Victoria, followed by the Duchess of

Sutherland and Lord Albermarle, stepped in. The door was closed and the eight white horses started off slowly on their trip around the city to Westminster Abbey.

A gun fired nearby was the signal to her people that the Queen was on her way. As she waved to the crowds lining the street, the sun broke through. The bands played, the people cheered, the stunningly uniformed soldiers marched, and the young girl's heart swelled with the overpowering emotion of the moment.

The coach passed slowly along between banks of spectators, thousands standing, some lucky enough to have seats in the stands, and others crowding together at windows and on rooftops. For the great majority, the coronation was a battle of wits and endurance. Those who came early and were not discouraged by the rain or the pushing of late-comers had a clear view. For the rest, it was every man for himself. Victoria smiled as she saw picnic baskets everywhere—on the arms of standees, in the laps of the seat holders. The most fortunate sight-seers, she knew, were those who sat in the seats erected in front of the clubs. They could wander in and out at will, enjoying delicious champagne lunches and break-fasts set up for them in the clubrooms, and yet not miss a moment of the pageant.

And so the procession wound along, the coaches filled with England's greatest men and visiting notables and accompanied by others on horseback. Victoria's regi-ments marched along in thrilling style to the martial music of the bands and the cheering of the crowds. A particularly loud roar reached the golden coach and the Queen guessed, rightly, that her people were applauding the Duke of Wellington, their greatest hero. A second and larger burst puzzled her. She found out later that it was for Marshal Soult, the French ambassador, whose coach followed Wellington's. In true British fashion the crowds showed their good sportsmanship by welcoming the man their hero had defeated in the Napoleonic wars.

The royal coach drew up to Westminster Abbey at about eleven-thirty and Victoria went directly into a robing room near the entrance. Her eight beautiful young train bearers were waiting for her and they all chattered excitedly as they helped her into the heavy velvet mantle with its deep ermine border. She thought, as they fluttered around her, how enchanting they looked in their gowns of white satin and silver tissue trimmed with pink roses. And how pretty their hair was with the wreaths of silver corn ears worn on the front, with pink roses encircling the plaits at the back.

When the mantle was in place the eight girls took their positions around it and lifted it from the floor. Lord Conyngham took hold of the very end of it and the procession left the little room and started up the long aisle. As soon as they had taken their first few steps Victoria realized that something was wrong; instead of walking smoothly the maids were jerkily out of step. She looked over her shoulder and saw what the trouble was. Their gowns had been made with long trains, the designer not taking into consideration the fact that their hands would be busy with the Queen's mantle. So, as they didn't have a third hand to hold their trains out of the way, the poor girls had to kick them awkwardly back out from under their feet as they took each step.

I must not let it bother me, resolved Victoria, and managed, somehow, to glide along like a lovely little swan. All eyes in the Abbey were on the tiny but stately figure wending its way with such dignity. Her whole being was absorbed in the desire and determination to carry out her part in the great day to perfection; but even in her concentration she could not help noticing how beautiful the banks of peers and peeresses looked in their velvet and fur robes, and how the peeresses' diamonds blazed in the lights as she passed them.

The procession reached the center of the Abbey and the ceremony began. Victoria was relieved to find Lord Melbourne stationed nearby and a bishop standing on each side of her. She was able to whisper questions to them from time to time, because the procedure had not been carefully rehearsed. Unfortunately the Bishops weren't too sure of it themselves and once they helped her out of her seat before a prayer was finished.

When the time came for the sacred robes, the Queen felt almost lost in them. They were so big and heavy! But the worst moment was when the Archbishop tried to put the special ring on her finger. It just wouldn't go on. Victoria flinched with pain. "You have the wrong finger," she whispered. "They measured the other one."

"No, no," insisted the Archbishop, "it has to go on this one," and he forced it on. The poor finger swelled and Victoria had to soak it in ice water later to get the ring off.

The moment the Queen was never to forget was when the crown was placed on her small, smooth head. The Abbey full of people broke into triumphant shouts, the drums rolled, the trumpets blew, and there was a great firing of guns to announce to the world that the Queen was crowned! Victoria, her hands holding the Scepter and the Orb, and her heart too full for a whispered word, looked at her beloved Prime Minister. Their eyes met, both pairs wet with tears. What a kind, what a fatherly look, thought the girl, who had never known the comfort and joy of sharing triumphs or sorrows with an understanding father.

Victoria was only dimly conscious of the fact that there was a great deal of commotion in the Abbey. She was told later that the odd, scrambling noise behind the throne was the page boys' snatching at the handfuls of coronation medals that were always tossed in the air at this point in the ceremony.

And something was going on among the peers and peeresses. A Lord Glenelg, well known for his habit of falling asleep in public, had drowsed off, wakened in time to put on his coronet in unison with the other peers, and then fallen asleep again. His heavy jeweled headpiece rolled off and disappeared under the seats. "Oh," he said loudly, "I have lost my nightcap!"

The laughter died down, the pages went back to their positions, and the peers proceeded to pay homage to their Queen. All went smoothly until eighty-two-year-old Lord Rolle lived up to his name and, missing the top step of the dais, rolled back down the other stairs in a tangle of white silk stockings, and velvet and ermine train. He did not seem to be hurt and rose to start back up again. Victoria left her throne hastily and descended the first two steps to meet him and receive his homage there. Her thoughtfulness caused a murmur of appreciation to run through the Abbey.

The great ceremony neared its close. The Queen felt more at ease now and managed to exchange smiles with Lehzen, who was watching her from a box just above the royal box occupied by the Duchess of Kent and other members of the family. Victoria's mother, undoubtedly desperately unhappy over the breach between herself and her daughter, wept so uncontrollably through the whole ceremony that her lady-in-waiting had to place her coronet on the bowed head and hold it there. Perhaps, due to her distress, she did not notice that her royal child had a smile, at this great moment, for the Prime Minister and her governess but not for her mother.

Before the procession re-formed, the Queen and her attendants and some of the other participants in the ceremony were escorted to St. Edward's Chapel. Victoria looked around in amazement. The chapel held a table loaded with sandwiches and bottles of wine. How odd, to eat in a chapel! But after the shock of the idea wore off, she was very glad to share in the much-needed refreshment and to see that Lord Melbourne, who was obviously exhausted by the emotional and physical strain of the day, had something to eat and drink.

When the repast was finished, the Queen was again handed the Orb and the Scepter and she and her retinue passed back down the long aisle of the cathedral. She found her mother and two of her aunts waiting for her in the robing room and they all rested for an hour before beginning the slow drive back to Buckingham Palace.

"I feel quite well," announced Victoria. "I hope the rest of the people in the Abbey are having something to eat and an opportunity to stretch their legs."

The gold coach and all the other gorgeous vehicles were drawing up to the Abbey entrance. The coachmen, who had lounged around in St. James's Park with their wigs off, smoking, eating, and chatting, now were back in their seats, the picture of formality. At four-thirty the Queen emerged, wearing her crown and carrying the royal regalia. She stepped into the coach, the horses were off, and the last half of the glorious procession was under way. It wound through the crowded streets until, just after six o'clock, it arrived finally at the great iron gates of Buckingham Palace and the Queen was home.

VI

Victoria Falls in Love

The crown was locked up in its special box and taken away, and the velvet robes were swathed in their long bags. The visitors were on their way home. Victoria stood at the window and watched a small army of workmen taking down the decorations. Life, she thought, should be fairly peaceful for a while.

The young Queen was right. Life was very peaceful all the rest of the summer and that winter. There were problems, of course, but nothing serious, and Victoria found plenty of time and energy to enjoy herself. Windsor was fun again. When the Court was at Buckingham Palace, there could be dancing almost every evening. The round music room, with its beautiful domed ceiling, its huge crystal chandeliers, and its long windows opening on the circular balcony, was an ideal place for musical parties and balls. It held either large or small groups quite comfortably and the servants became accustomed to taking up the rugs and waxing the floor for the Queen's pleasure.

The cold weather passed, the trees turned a soft green, and the hedges bloomed. Another birthday—Victoria sighed as she turned the pages of her calendar. Her peace of mind had disappeared with the gay, giddy winter and she hated to think about either of the two problems that were bothering her.

The first was a personal matter. Leopold was pressing his niece to come to a decision about marrying Albert of Saxe-Coburg-Gotha. Victoria paced restlessly up and down her sitting room as she considered the question. Why *should* she have to marry so young? For that matter, why should she have to marry at all? Queen Elizabeth never did. Besides, she thought, why should her Uncle Leopold assume that she was more or less betrothed to Albert? She had liked him well enough when they met, but that was years before and they were really only children then. She had changed and he probably had, too. She was grown up now and was Queen, and she liked things the way they were. A husband might spoil everything!

The truth of the matter was that Victoria was tired. She had worked and played too hard the last few months. And she was aware that she wasn't as popular with her people as she had been when she first came to the throne; why this was, she would find out sometime later. Perhaps a marriage with a German prince would make matters worse; she knew only too well how much her uncles had been hated by the English public. But if she decided against Albert, and she had to marry, who should it be?

Her Uncle Billy's choice for her had been the Prince of Orange. Victoria remembered how angry King Leopold had been when he heard this, and she smiled to herself as she thought of the way everyone at Court still watched her whenever the Prince was with her. There was the time she went to a window to see him ride away from Windsor Castle, a rather startling figure in a bright red uniform and a hat with green plumes. "How like a radish he looks!" she said to the lady nearest her, realizing quite well that this unromantic remark would quiet the rumors that she was falling in love with the young Dutchman.

When Victoria was still a princess, she had had one real beau. Young Lord Elphinstone, William IV's handsome, charming, and well-born Lord of the Bedchamber, had fallen deeply in love with her—so much in love that he would sit and stare at her in church every Sunday. She still had a sketch he had made of her during the sermon one time. Victoria sighed to herself. Well, it was a good thing she hadn't lost her heart, too. She knew now that the King had done a wise thing in sending him off to India to be Governor of Madras, but it seemed very cruel at the time. And he had been a good governor for seven years, despite his youth and inexperience.

Should she send for him to come home? No, it would not do to choose an Englishman for her Consort. There would be too much jealousy among the families of all the other eligible young men; Lord Melbourne agreed with her, she knew.

So the little Queen tried to put the whole matter out of her mind for a while. But the Court noticed how often the table conversation crept around to matrimony.

Finally, one day in April, she mustered up her courage and had a talk with the Prime Minister. For some reason she felt terrified—foolishly, as she confided to her diary that night. For how could she be frightened talking to *him?*

"It is King Leopold's great wish that I marry Albert," she told him, "but I cannot decide anything until I see the Prince again."

"That's the only way," agreed Lord Melbourne. "How would it be with the Duchess?"

"You need have no fear whatever on that score," answered the Queen.

"Cousins are not very good things," said the Minister thoughtfully, "and those Coburgs are not popular abroad; the Russians hate them."

"Who is there else?" asked Victoria. They went over the list of possibilities. "None of them would do." She was very firm. "For myself," she added, "at present, *my* feeling is quite against ever marrying."

Lord Melbourne looked thoughtful. "It's a great change in the situation. It's a very serious thing, as it concerns both the political effect and your own happiness."

"Albert has advantages over the other princes you have mentioned," admitted the Queen, "although he is a few months younger than I am. And Uncle Leopold is pressing me a great deal on the subject."

"Well," continued the Prime Minister, more or less thinking aloud, "if one was to make a man for it, one would hardly know what to make; he mustn't be stupid —nor cunning."

The second problem, the increasing political unrest and probability of a change in government, came to a head a few days after this discussion and drove everything else out of Victoria's mind. The young Queen knew perfectly well that she was supposed to stand aside and not dabble in politics; the Crown, of course, should show no political bias. But how could she bear to have another Prime Minister in place of Lord Melbourne, her right hand, her second father, her friend and teacher?

Matters seemed to be reaching a crisis and Victoria's heart grew heavier and heavier. It was a rather grim-faced little monarch who granted Sir Robert Peel an audience one April day. Peel, the head of his party, had decided to settle a few matters with the Queen. He named the men who, in his opinion, should take over the important positions in Victoria's household when the government changed hands. The Queen protested a bit, then grudgingly conceded that her men would have to give way to them.

"And now," said Peel, "about the ladies—"

Victoria drew herself up to what height she could manage. "My ladies will, of course, remain with me," she announced firmly. "I will give up my gentlemen if necessary, but not my ladies."

Sir Robert was aghast. The more he argued, the more determinedly Victoria stood her ground. He left the Royal Presence an angry and bewildered man. Such a thing had never happened before! Meetings were called, letters written, interviews sought. Every possible source of pressure was brought to bear on the Queen, but she *would not give up her ladies.* Suddenly the battle was over. Peel and his party concluded that her stand would be interpreted as a vote of no confidence in them and they decided to wait for a more propitious time to take over the reins.

It was a happy girl who summoned Lord Melbourne and talked everything over later that day, and wrote the news of her triumph to her Uncle Leopold. His answer approved of her stand, assuring her that she had acted wisely. She thought so, too; but sixty years later, the weathered and withered survivor of many such storms, she wasn't so sure. "I was very young then," she said to her private secretary, "and perhaps I should act differently if it was all to be done again."

The English people had felt for some time that she was favoring the Whigs too much and this was proof of it to them. Victoria had been correct earlier that spring when she felt that she wasn't as popular as she had been with her subjects, and this was one of the reasons. Another was that too much had been made of the young Queen's love of dancing and balls, and not enough of the sober way she worked at her desk. But the blackest mark against her was that she handled a Court scandal so clumsily that a young girl's reputation was ruined. The maid-in-waiting was proved to be completely innocent of the charge made against her, and the Queen's part in the affair, though due to her youth and inexperience in such matters, was never forgiven or forgotten.

Victoria's twentieth birthday arrived and the Queen felt very grown up as she said farewell to her teens. That night she sat at her desk, with her diary open before her, and counted her blessings. "I feel," she wrote, "I owe more to *two* people than I can ever repay! My dear Lehzen, and my dear excellent Lord Melbourne."

June passed quietly, and most of July, but Victoria was still fretting about her situation in regard to Prince Albert. She had finally agreed that he and his brother Ernest should come to visit her sometime that fall and she dreaded it.

"Don't you think," she said, looking hopefully at Lord Melbourne, "that there is a feeling around that too many of my relatives have been to England this year? Perhaps I should postpone their visit."

"No," answered Lord Melbourne, "I have heard nothing of the sort mentioned by anyone."

Victoria looked depressed. "The whole subject is odious to me," she complained. "I hate to decide about it. There is no engagement between us, but Albert knows that there is a possibility of our union. It isn't right to keep him on, but I can't decide before they come!"

Lord Melbourne smiled at the worried little face. He took her hand and patted it comfortingly. "If I were you," he suggested, "I would have it clearly understood before the Prince arrives here that you can't do anything for a year."

"It is disagreeable for me to see him, though," replied the Queen.

A few days later she took her Minister's advice and wrote a long, firm letter to her Uncle Leopold in which she said:

> I am anxious to put several questions to you, and to mention feelings of mine upon the subject of my cousins' visit, which I am desirous should not transpire. First of all, I wish to know if *Albert* is aware of the wish of his *Father* and *you* relative to *me*? Secondly, if he knows that there is *no engagement* between us? I am anxious that you should acquaint Uncle Ernest, if I should like Albert, that I can make *no final promise this year*, for, at the *very earliest*, any such event could not take place till *two* or *three* years *hence*. For, independent of my youth, and my *great* repugnance to change my present position, there is *no anxiety* evinced in this country for such an event, and it would be more prudent,

in my opinion, to wait till such demonstration is shown. . . .

Though all the reports of Albert are most favorable, and though I have little doubt I shall like him, still one can never answer beforehand for *feelings,* and I may not have the *feeling* for him which is requisite to ensure happiness. I *may* like him as a friend, and as a *cousin,* and as a *brother,* but not *more;* and should this be the case (which is not likely), I am *very* anxious that it be understood that I am not guilty of any breach of promise, for I *never gave any.* I am sure you will understand my anxiety, for I should otherwise, were this not completely understood, be in a very painful position. As it is, I am rather nervous about the visit, for the subject I allude to is not an agreeable one to me. I have little else to say, dear Uncle, as I have now spoken openly to you, which I was very, *very anxious* to do.

Victoria finished the letter and read it over, picking up her pen from time to time to underline another word or two, a bad habit she had learned from Leopold himself. Then she sealed it and gave a sigh of relief. She had done all she could and now she must try not to worry about the matter.

Prince Albert, in Germany, was as unhappy about all this uncertainty as was Victoria. He knew that from the moment he was born on August twenty-sixth, 1819—looking, said his grandmother, "like a little squirrel"—he had been destined to marry his Cousin Victoria. It was the dearest hope and dream of both branches of the family that the "May Blossom" would someday be the wife of the "little squirrel."

As the English princess was brought up to be a queen, so Albert was brought up to be a queen's consort. He was a beautiful baby and a delightful little boy. He, like Victoria, had his moments of rebellion and insubordination, but he was easily molded into a model prince. He was intelligent, affectionate, and determined to do a good job in the position in which Fate had placed him.

He grew up in a small yellow stone castle at Rosenau, and he loved it with all his heart. Looking out of its windows, he reveled in the beautiful gardens full of roses; the nearby woods with their beeches, elms, and oaks; and the river and waterfall gleaming in the sun. It was a restful and lovely view, always, as it spread out to peaceful fields and then up a hillside to a dark pine forest. He and his brother Ernest had tutors, then went to the famous University of Bonn, and finally completed their education by traveling all over Europe. Ernest, as the oldest son, would, of course, inherit the duchy and take his place as the ruler of Saxe-Coburg-Gotha. He was like his father and most of the European royalty of the day; he liked wine, women, and song and spent most of his time enjoying himself. Albert was completely different. He hated weakness or indulgence of any kind and was as moral as his brother was immoral. He was ambitious and full of intellectual curiosity. He wanted to know just what had made the world the way it was, and he was eager to contribute his share toward improving it.

From the day Victoria ascended the throne, Albert had been marking time. He could not settle on a career until he knew whether that contrary young girl over in England was going to marry him or not. A prince could not propose to a queen, so he had to wait for her to make up her mind. As he wrote to his best friend, he simply wanted the matter settled one way or the other. He had no objection to their wedding being postponed for two or three years. But he didn't want to spend all that time in doubt and then be told there would be no marriage. He realized only too well that being Prince Consort of the Queen of Great Britain would be extremely difficult. But he also knew that as Prince Consort he would be in a position to work for the good of humanity.

As the summer waned, Victoria grew more and more nervous. Albert did, too. Marriage, in those days, was for life. Divorce or separation rarely occurred—almost never in royal families. While Victoria talked over her future with Lord Melbourne or brooded about it when she should have been sleeping, that was what worried her most. "I *must* make the right decision," she told herself. "If I marry, my marriage must always set an example for my people to follow. It isn't enough for my husband and me to love each other. And I must be sure to choose the right father for the next ruler of England."

King Leopold, who had been so anxious for their union, stayed in Belgium and did all he could to bring the story to a happy ending. He kept in touch with the girl and the boy and arranged for Albert to visit him on his way to England. This gave Victoria the opportunity to put off the dreaded meeting a little longer. She wrote her uncle and asked him, if there was talk of the Coburgs arriving at Windsor by the thirtieth of September, to please hold them up a day or two as she had a group of Ministers coming to confer with her on that date. "It might look," she said, "as if the Ministers were there to settle matters if Albert came when they were there."

Leopold's answer arrived and Victoria tore it open with nervous fingers. She read it, then looked up with a surprised and rather annoyed expression. The Coburgs couldn't arrive before October the sixth! Well! She flounced a bit as she left the room. If Leopold could have seen the success of his little maneuver, he would have been well pleased. It was a sound move to let the Queen see that she was not the only reluctant one of the pair.

October the sixth arrived, and no visitors. October the seventh, eighth, ninth . . . then the tenth dawned. It was a Thursday and it started off very badly for Victoria, as the wave of unpopularity that she was suffering came to a climax with someone throwing stones through the windows of her private apartments.

As she dressed and ate her breakfast, she tried to

steady herself. "I must forget this," she told herself. "Albert should arrive today and I must not seem upset." How the day dragged—noon, afternoon, teatime; still no sign of the travelers.

Victoria had just finished dressing for dinner when a servant knocked on the door with the word that the Coburgs were driving up to the castle. She hastened to the top of the staircase leading down into the Great Hall and there they stood. The Queen's heart began to beat in a very odd fashion. She looked at Albert. Albert looked at his little cousin. Why, she thought, he is *beautiful!*

Lord Melbourne turned to her at the table, after looking up and down the seated diners. "Where are our visitors?" he asked.

The Queen laughed and tried to sound just as usual. "The poor boys," she explained, "are eating dinner in their rooms. Their luggage hasn't arrived." She tried to turn the talk to the usual topics, but it always came back to her cousins. Lord Melbourne's heart sank. He knew his little monarch so well! He didn't have to be a mind reader to realize why she was so gay tonight and why she looked so pretty. This was not the nervous, unhappy girl he had talked to earlier in the day. He looked at the flushed face beside him and tried to be merry, too. But his Queen had been his own Queen in a special, dear way and he saw already that she was slipping away from him.

Albert and Ernest joined the party after dinner and Victoria presented them proudly to her Minister and the other ladies and gentlemen. "Come and sit beside me, Ernest," she commanded, making room for him on the sofa. Lord Melbourne joined in their chat, but he watched how the Queen's eyes kept straying over to where Prince Albert sat. He had to admit that, as far as appearances went, Albert made all the other eligible princes look like ugly ducklings.

Victoria's head was in a happy whirl. Was there ever such a Prince Charming as Albert? He was so tall and he had such a beautiful figure, with its wide shoulders and thin waist. It would be fun to describe him in her diary; to write of his wavy brown hair, his blue eyes—yes, his exquisite nose and mouth! Even his delicate mustachios and slight, but slight whiskers.

There was a ball in honor of the princes the next evening and the Queen wore her prettiest frock. She sighed with delight as she danced with Albert, for he was a graceful dancer and looked completely stunning in his full-dress uniform. The young couple did the gallop together, and danced quadrilles; but poor Victoria had to sit on the side lines and watch as he waltzed with her lucky ladies. "Never mind," she told herself, "perhaps sometime soon . . ."

Albert came to her side when the waltz ended. The tiny queen smiled shyly at him. "You have no flower in your buttonhole," she said, pulling one out of her bouquet.

"As a matter of fact," answered Albert, "I have no buttonhole. But we will fix that." Before she could protest he had taken out a pocket knife, cut a slit in his uniform, and tucked the blossom proudly in place.

He was "dearest Albert" in her journal that night, and by Sunday she confessed to Lord Melbourne that seeing him had made her change her mind about marrying. "Take another week," suggested her Prime Minister. But Victoria was slipping deeper in love every hour and his advice fell on deaf ears. She was feeling a bit silly about that long letter to her Uncle Leopold, and quite ashamed of the months of uncertainty through which she had put Albert. Suppose she had lost him as a result of her shilly-shallying?

On Monday morning the brothers went out shooting and Victoria, rather timidly, took advantage of their absence to have a longer talk with Lord Melbourne. "I've made up my mind," she said after an awkward pause.

"You have?" Her Minister knew only too well what she meant. "Well, then, about the time?"

"Oh, not for a year, I think," replied the Queen, blushing.

"That's too long," said Melbourne. "Parliament will have to be assembled to make a provision for the Prince and the less time there is for everyone to think up objections and to talk the better. Though I don't think there'll be much; on the contrary," he went on, with tears in his eyes, "I think it'll be well received. I hear there is an anxiety now it should be, and I'm very glad of it. I think it is a good thing and you'll be more comfortable. A woman cannot stand alone for long."

After they had discussed the matter a little longer, Victoria took his hand and thanked him for being so kind to her. How fatherly he is, she thought. I must remember all the good things he said and put them in my journal. But she did not notice the sad droop of his shoulders as he left the room, for the little sunflower was turning her head to a new sun and Lord Melbourne's day was over.

The Prime Minister managed a private word with the Queen after dinner that evening, telling her he had discussed her marriage with Lord Russell, an important and influential man in the Whig government, immediately after their morning talk. "Lord Russell feels that not too many people should know of your decision between the time you settle it with Albert and the announcement is made to the Privy Council. Probably just your immediate families."

Victoria agreed. "I will be glad to have it settled," she admitted. "I must confess that I have not been able to sleep the last few nights. And Albert"—her voice caressed his name—"tells me he has had the same trouble."

She went to bed that night determined to have her important talk with her suitor as early as possible the next day. She found that the other sleepless nights were as nothing compared with this one. She went over and over what she must say to Albert. "How can I do it?" she asked herself. "How can I bear to propose to a man?" Her face flushed in the darkness and she turned restlessly from side to side. Like every other girl she knew, she had been brought up to be modest and shy in the presence of the other sex. If she were one of her ladies-in-waiting, she would be expected to faint or run to her mother at the first sign of a proposal.

At last it was morning and Victoria went down to breakfast. Her cousins had gone out hunting early, she was told, and she sighed with relief. But the reprieve was a short one; she was standing at the window a short time later when suddenly there they were, charging up the hill to the castle at a rapid pace. She took her courage in both small, shaking hands and sent a message to Albert asking him to come to her sitting room as soon as possible.

The door opened and Victoria's Prince Charming walked in. The young couple were alone for the first time. The tiny Queen looked down at the tips of her slippers and patted her skirt nervously as she tried to start the conversation. It was several minutes before she managed to say, in a trembling low voice, "I think you must be aware of why I wished you to come here—you have won my whole heart—it would make me *too happy* if you would consent to what I wish—"

Albert stepped quickly forward and interrupted the shy little speech by taking the scared young woman in his arms. Victoria stopped being a queen and was just a happy girl, madly in love, returning the kisses of her tall, handsome sweetheart.

When they came out of the rosy clouds sometime later, they found there was much to discuss. They both realized the seriousness of the step they were taking, and the difficulties that lay before them. "I know I'm not worthy of you," protested Victoria, "and you are making a great sacrifice. Being a Prince Consort will be a hard task."

Albert looked down on the bowed, smooth brown head. "I am the unworthy one," he assured her firmly, "and being married to you will more than make up for any sacrifices."

The Queen gave a great, happy sigh. She had said all the difficult things that had to be said. She raised her eyes to the tender eyes above her and crept back into the heaven of her lover's arms.

VII

A Royal Bride

Victoria and Albert went down to luncheon trying to look as if nothing had happened. But every time their eyes met, a lovely pink flush spread over the girl's face and she found it difficult to converse calmly with her table partners. How wonderfully Albert hides his feelings in public, she thought. I hope I'm doing it half as well.

Later that afternoon the newly betrothed couple found time to write their good news to those most entitled to share the secret. Albert wanted his father and grandmother to hear as soon as possible and, when he had finished those two letters, he couldn't resist dashing off a love note to his little sweetheart. "Oh, that I may succeed in making you very, very happy, as happy as you deserve to be," and he signed it "in body and soul ever your slave, Your loyal Albert."

Victoria, in another room, was smiling as she took up

her pen. How pleased Uncle Leopold would be to open *this* letter! How right he had been in choosing Albert for her and how sorry she was to have worried him with all her doubts and fears during the summer.

She wrote firmly:

> My mind is quite made up and I told Albert this morning of it. . . . He seems *perfection,* and I think I have the prospect of great happiness before me. I *love* him more than I can say, and I shall do everything in my power to render the sacrifice he has made (for sacrifice in my opinion it is) as small as I can. . . . My feelings are a *little* changed, I must say, since last Spring, when I said I couldn't *think* of marrying for *three* or *four* years; but seeing Albert has changed all this.

Victoria now discovered how wonderful it is to be young and in love with the right man. She woke up every morning anticipating the happy hours ahead in which to enjoy her lover's company, and retired to her bed at night to dream about the happenings of the day. The young couple rode and danced and romped with Eos, Albert's pet greyhound, who always traveled with him. They sang duets together, and trios with Ernest. Victoria watched the two brothers play chess in the evenings and wished she were clever enough to play, too. Then the weather turned cool and Albert and his bride-to-be managed to steal an hour now and then to sit before the fire and plan their wedding and their future together. Early February was the time set for the ceremony and it was exciting to settle some of the details.

The sad day of farewells arrived much too soon. "Do not repine, my Liebchen," Albert comforted his wet-eyed sweetheart. "The time will pass and then we will be together for always."

Victoria expected the time to drag, but she discovered that there was a great deal to be done in the less than three months before her wedding. On the twenty-third of November she dressed in a simple morning frock; clasped a bracelet with a miniature of Albert painted on it around her wrist, to give herself courage; and went to make the declaration of her coming marriage to her council.

The young Queen kept her voice clear and steady, but her hands trembled noticeably. Oh, dear, she thought, why did they write the declaration on this thin onion-skin paper? It is shaking so I can hardly read it.

"It must have been a nervous thing to do," said the Duchess of Gloucester afterward.

"It was a much more nervous thing when I proposed to Prince Albert!" answered Victoria.

With that formality over, there were many decisions to be made. Lord Melbourne brought the records of other royal marriages and he and his little Queen went over them together. "Where would you like the ceremony to be held?" he asked her.

"I have been thinking that the Chapel Royal in St.

James's Palace would be best. We can limit the number of guests there and it is not too long a drive from Buckingham."

"Yes, I think you are right. If it were held at Westminster Abbey it would resemble your coronation too much. I have the Peerage here," he added, holding up the official list of the nobility. "You must choose your bridesmaids as soon as possible."

Victoria sighed. The question of bridesmaids brought with it the thought of their gowns, and that reminded her of the trousseau she must select and the fittings she must endure between now and February. She turned to Lord Melbourne. "You must see that I do not neglect my other duties during this busy time," she said.

The Queen was, of course, never too busy to write to Albert and she found it very soothing to pour out her heart to him. The mail from abroad was often slow in arriving and she waited for his letters with all the patience she could manage. They were so worth waiting for—and how she read and reread them! One of her favorites began:

> Dearly beloved Victoria, I long to talk to you; otherwise the separation is too painful. Your dear picture stands on my table in front of me, and I can hardly take my eyes off it. I can sometimes imagine you are answering me and the thought makes me most happy. . . . What a delight it must be to walk through the whole of my life, with its joys and

storms, with you by my side! Where love is, there is happiness. Love of you fills my whole heart.

Dearest Albert, she thought as she put it down and took up another, how dear, how perfect he is, and she bloomed with joy as she read on.

"Our lips," wrote her prince, "will blossom afresh when they touch each other. Each day that flies by brings me nearer to you; soon we shall be in each other's arms. With burning love for you . . . farewell, dearest Victoria, I kiss you a thousand times." Her cheeks were quite pink when she tucked that one away and opened another that ended with the loving words "Dearest, deeply loved Victoria, the angel who will illumine my life . . . all my thoughts have been with you and your image fills my whole soul . . . may your dear heart be my dwelling place."

However, as Victoria had often heard, the course of true love seldom runs smoothly; the young couple had their disagreements. Albert wanted to choose his own staff, and he was naturally distressed when Victoria answered that she knew better than he did whom he should have—and went ahead and arranged the matter without consulting him further. Then, when the question of their honeymoon arose, Albert wrote that he felt they should have at least a week or two by themselves at Windsor. Victoria replied in a smug little letter that she was Queen and could "not stay in seclusion more than two or three days."

Another thing that disturbed the Prince was that the allowance voted him as Prince Consort was not so generous as it should have been, and this made him feel that perhaps he was not going to be too welcome in England. All these difficulties and disagreements made the young couple unhappy for a time, but each obstacle was surmounted in its turn. As Albert wrote, after one problem was solved, "Today there is nothing to upset me and I can tell you with a free heart how inexpressibly I love you."

As Victoria went through the busy days she tried to picture what her betrothed was doing and thinking in faraway Germany. She knew how dearly he loved his family and his home and what a painful thing it was going to be to leave them. Once he was Prince Consort of England he would have few opportunities to go back to Rosenau, the home of his heart. Queens and their husbands do not have much time to travel for pleasure.

Soon it was time to send General Gray with three carriages to Germany to escort the bridegroom and his suite to London. Victoria saw the General before he left and entrusted him with the Order of the Garter for Albert. It is the greatest honor the Queen of England can bestow on anyone and, as Albert's father was already a knight of the order, he could be authorized to invest his son.

Prince Ernest, happy over his son's approaching marriage but sad over losing him, followed the Garter ceremony with a farewell banquet for a hundred and eighty members of the Court of Coburg. The dinner was a great success but it almost ended in tragedy. With the drinking of the final toast, a window was thrown open as a signal for a volley of shots to be fired outside the castle. The wind blew a thin curtain into a candle flame and it blazed to the ceiling. Fortunately nothing else caught fire and the scare was soon over.

Prince Albert watched the heavy luggage go into one of the carriages and gave Eos a pat as she was settled in to ride with it. Then he turned and joined his father and brother; General Gray and the rest of the gentlemen took their places, and the cavalcade was off. Germany was cold and snowy and the roads were anything but smooth, so they could not make very good speed. From time to time Albert would get a glimpse of his dog's head at the window of the baggage carrier and it reminded him of a joke he and Ernest played on the people of Coburg one fine day. The two young princes had been riding along between lanes of applauding subjects when they suddenly ducked down and held Eos up to receive the adulation!

Albert sighed as he remembered how gay that ride was. He knew that they were nearing his grandmother's home, where he must make a farewell visit, and he dreaded the sad, inevitable scene. He knew she must realize, as he did, that they might never meet again. By the time the carriages arrived at her door, she had, indeed, worked herself up into a frenzy of grief; and when

Albert finally tore himself away after a last kiss, she hung out of the window watching the cortege disappear, holding out her arms despairingly, and crying "Albert, Albert!" in heartbroken tones.

The Prince tried to seem normal and cheerful, but the parting with his grandmother and the knowledge that he would soon cross over the border and leave his Fatherland were almost too much for him. The frontier was just ahead and he could see that something had been arranged there in his honor. As the carriages drove up, they found themselves under a farewell arch of fir trees and surrounded by a cluster of shivering young girls, in thin muslin frocks, carrying garlands of roses and trying to sing through their chattering teeth. Their obvious discomfort made Albert forget his own woes and the worst part of his ordeal was over.

The travelers had a rough crossing and were more than glad to see Dover's cliffs. Despite a cold, driving rain there were enthusiastic crowds waiting to greet the Queen's husband-to-be and their heartening welcome did much to raise Albert's spirits. A good dinner, a fire, and a warm bed at Canterbury helped, too, and it was a happy and eager bridegroom who started off for London the next day. The carriage containing the luggage and Albert's dog went right on through, and so Victoria, waiting impatiently for her sweetheart's arrival, found herself greeting the first of his suite—Eos!

The wedding was scheduled for Monday, February

the tenth, and at four-thirty on the preceding Saturday the carriages with Albert and his party, complete with military escort, drove through the center gate of the palace and up to the great door. Victoria had heard that they were approaching and, with heart beating wildly, was waiting just inside. She saw Prince Ernest step out first, then his father, then Albert. He looks beautiful—and so well, she thought as she flew into his arms for an ecstatic hug.

Victoria woke up on her wedding day and stretched happily. She felt wonderful. And to think that just a few days ago she had been so tired and nervous that she had told Lord Melbourne she thought she had the measles. Dear Lord Melbourne, how kind he was and how he had soothed her and helped her over all the difficulties! What a good joke he had made about the new coat he was having tailored for the wedding! "It is like building a seventy-four-gun ship," he had boasted. "No one will look at the bride!"

She jumped out of bed and looked out of the window. The sky was gray and threatening, but there was no use fussing—and English skies do clear suddenly, sometimes. She rang for her breakfast and began to dress. The door opened and in came Lehzen with a pretty ring, and her mother with a nosegay of orange blossoms.

"Now I really believe it is my wedding day," she said as she sniffed the fragrant flowers.

After breakfast was over she shooed everyone out of

the room and wrote her last two notes as a single girl, one to Lord Melbourne and one to her husband-so-soon-to-be.

Dearest

How are you today, and have you slept well? I have rested very well and feel very comfortable today. What weather! I believe, however, the rain will cease.

Send one word when you, my most dearly loved bridegroom, will be ready.

Thy ever faithful,
VICTORIA R.

As soon as the notes were sent off, the hairdresser arrived and took a long time arranging the silky hair and carefully fastening the wreath of orange blossoms in place. There was a knock on the door. Albert! Again everyone was sent out of the room. And, as she wrote in her diary later, she had a moment with him "for the *last* time *alone*, as my *bridegroom*."

The Prince went on his way and it was time for the wedding veil and the ornaments. How glad I am, thought Victoria, that everything I am wearing today was made in my dear England. The dress was of specially woven Spitalsfield silk trimmed with a deep flounce and bertha collar of an English lace called Honitan. The veil was of the same lace and her long kid gloves were of English leather and made in London.

French gloves were the fashion but this bride was not wearing them. As a final touch Victoria fastened on a diamond necklace; then Albert's wedding present, a diamond and sapphire brooch; and, finally, the wide blue ribbon of the Order of the Garter.

Victoria waited for the word that Albert and his suite had arrived at St. James's and that the carriages had returned for her and her party. She suddenly found herself in tears—tears that would not stop flowing. She dabbed at them frantically with a handkerchief. "I must not let them drop on my dress," she told herself. "I'm sure this silk would spot."

Lord Uxbridge entered to escort her down the three long flights of stairs and her mother followed close behind him. Victoria had the tears under control by this time, but her eyes were pink and swollen and she wished desperately that she were an ordinary bride with her wedding veil over her face. But royal brides belong to their people and they would want to see her face, so the veil had to fall back on her shoulders.

The stairs and halls were lined with spectators. They had clapped enthusiastically when Albert wended his way to his carriage; now, at sight of the young Queen, they broke into loud acclamations. She walked through them more hurriedly than usual and kept her head shyly down.

It was twelve-fifteen when she stepped into her coach, followed by her mother and the Duchess of Sutherland. Five other carriages were filled with the rest of her household, and the cortege, escorted by the Household Cavalry, started at a snail's pace for St. James's Palace. The band struck up "God Save the Queen" and a tremendous shout went up from the crowds.

The streets had been filled with people since early morning. Some stood on chairs and tables, some climbed trees, and some even paid enormous sums for good positions along the way. Despite the discomfort of the sharp showers and the crowding, the mass of onlookers were good-natured. The English are sentimental at heart and their Queen was making a love match. Nothing could dampen their spirits and some of them even started a marrow-bone and cleaver concert in honor of the day.

As the royal carriages passed slowly by, all eyes were on the small white-veiled figure with serious face. Victoria, looking into the cheering crowds, felt even more deeply the solemnity of the step she was about to take. A fleeting smile or two crossed her countenance as she saw funny things happen along the way, but those smiles were rare.

The short ride was soon over and Victoria stepped out of her coach into the palace entrance and was ushered into a small chamber behind the Throne Room. There stood her twelve young maids of honor, waiting for her. They looked extremely lovely in their simple white gowns trimmed with white roses. The bridal procession was formed and the Queen waited for the signal to start. Victoria's uncle, the Duke of Sussex, was to give her away. He stepped to her side.

"Are all the guests here?" asked Victoria.

"The palace is full," answered the Duke. "I hear they began arriving by nine o'clock this morning. They have put rows of seats on both sides of all the rooms we proceed through as well as in the chapel itself. Ah, there is the signal."

Victoria placed a shaking hand on her uncle's arm and the procession started. Her eyes tended to look down at the rich carpet laid through the palace in honor of the occasion, but she lifted them often enough to appreciate the colorful scene around her. The seats were cushioned in crimson and edged with gold fringe. The women wore gowns of almost every imaginable color, and most of them had wedding favors—white ribbons tied in bows, some with orange blossoms and layers of silver lace. The men brightened up their more somber garb with sprigs of the bridal flower.

A buzz and babble of comment broke out in each room as the cortege passed through to the next one; as it entered the chapel itself, there was such noise in the adjoining chamber that the attendants closed the door for a moment and demanded silence.

Victoria walked slowly up the chapel aisle; but now she was not aware of the purple and gold carpet, the elaborate gold cornice over the richly draped altar. She was only vaguely conscious of the Archbishops of York and Canterbury and the Bishop of London standing there beside it. Her eyes passed quickly over the familiar face of Aunt Adelaide standing near one of the four state chairs which would be occupied by her, the Duchess of Kent, the bride, and the groom. As her eyes found what they were seeking, the small white face flushed rosily and the Duke of Sussex had to adjust his step to a break in the rhythm of her walk.

For there stood Albert, waiting for his bride. Victoria's heart was full of love as she saw him there, so tall, so handsome in his field marshal's uniform, looking at her with such a protective, earnest expression on his dear face. Oh, she thought as she knelt to pray, I have so much to thank God for at this moment. All heads bent with the veiled one, then Victoria and the assembly sat down for a short period of quiet waiting. It was obvious that the Duchess of Kent was emotionally upset by the occasion—and so was Lord Melbourne, stationed nearby with the Sword of State.

The bride rose and Albert stepped to her side. They walked to the altar and the ceremony began, the young couple making their responses in clear, firm, carrying tones. Victoria raised her eyes for a second to the Prince's when she promised to obey; that bit of the service, sometimes omitted, had been left in at her particular request. When the groom placed the plain, thick gold ring on her finger, the waiting gunners outside the palace fired a royal salute and Victoria's heart jumped with happiness.

The pair were pronounced man and wife and there was a pleasant moment of informality as the members of the family clustered around them with kisses and congratulations. Victoria noticed Aunt Adelaide standing back, with her usual modesty. The new bride crossed immediately to her aunt's side and gave her an affectionate embrace.

The leading "actors" in the happy scene then took their places and returned as they had entered—except that, as the Queen recorded later in her diary, "my beloved Albert led me out." The groom held his bride's hand in such a way that everyone could see the ring, and the applause was deafening as the procession wound its way through the palace. The register was signed and the party retired to the Queen's Closet behind the Throne Room. There followed a delightful few minutes of admiring and excited chatter as the bride gave each bridesmaid a gold brooch studded with turquoises, in the form of an eagle.

The wedding party poured into the waiting carriages and, as the newly married pair stepped into theirs, the sun came out. Their smiles were sunny, too, and it was a radiant face that the Queen turned to her people on this return trip.

When they entered the Throne Room at Buckingham Palace, Lord Melbourne was there to welcome them and to turn them over to the throngs of nobility, children as well as grownups, waiting to wish them joy. When that duty was done, the couple slipped away to Victoria's dressing room for half an hour's rest before the wedding banquet.

Victoria turned to Albert as they sat side by side on

her little sofa. "I wanted Lord Melbourne on my left at the table, but he tells me that must be my uncle's seat as he gave me away. So let us make an opportunity to have a private chat with him before we go—and to praise his wonderful coat!"

The clock struck two-thirty and it was time to go down to the banquet hall. Three pages lifted Victoria's long satin train and she entered the room on the arm of her husband. The speeches, the food, the cutting of the three-hundred-pound cake, all seemed like a dream to the little bride. Ah, at last it was time to retire and change into her traveling costume, a white satin coat trimmed with swansdown and a white satin bonnet decked with orange blossoms.

It was about a quarter to four when Albert, now in a dark suit, joined his bride and they made their way to where the carriage waited to take them to Windsor for their short honeymoon. Lord Melbourne stood watching them. Victoria drew him to one side for a special farewell.

"Everything went so well," he assured her with tears in his eyes. "God bless you, ma'am."

The sun was out in real earnest now; the skies had turned a clear blue. Albert looked at the crowds lining the streets as their carriage started on its way.

"They will make a night of it, I expect," he said.

"I am so happy that I want everyone to be happy, too," answered the Queen. "I wish I could be sure that all my people will have a good dinner tonight and a glass of beer to drink to our health. We have arranged it for six hundred of the poor at Windsor, anyway."

London was soon left behind and the carriages rolled through the countryside. The roads there were lined with merrymakers, too, and gay with flowers, flags, and decorations. It was dark by the time they reached Eton and they found it a fairyland of special illuminations, filled with a surging mass of schoolboys and masters to cheer them on their way.

Windsor had been waiting impatiently for hours, stirred up by many false rumors of their imminent arrival. It was six-thirty before the townspeople saw a flight of rockets go up over Eton and heard the bells peal out their welcome.

The carriages came into sight, the Queen bowing and smiling and her groom receiving his share of the plaudits with high spirits. The crowds cheered and cheered. The cortege turned into the great castle courtyard and drew up at the entrance. Victoria, a bit stiff after the slow ride, stepped out of the carriage. She placed her small hand on her beloved Albert's arm and stepped over the threshold. The heavy door closed behind them—as the Queen wrote later in her journal, "I and Albert, alone."

VIII

Ten Happy Years

Albert strode down the palace hall, his legs looking like long black stilts. Victoria hurried desperately after him. Oh, dear, she thought, how angry he is! She trotted even faster and reached the door of her husband's room a second after he did, just in time to have it close in her face and to hear an unusual sound—a key turn in the lock.

A look of shocked incredulity spread over her face. Albert had locked her out! She stood there for a moment, then took an indignant step forward and rapped loudly.

"Who is it?" asked Albert.

Victoria drew her mouth into a straight line. "The Queen of England!" she answered, and waited for the door to open. It didn't. Again her fist banged on the door.

"Who is there?" asked Albert.

"The Queen." She rattled the knob impatiently. The door remained closed.

Knock, knock, knock—but more gently this time. "Who is there?" came the same question.

"Your wife, Albert," replied a subdued little voice. The key turned in the lock again and a repentant young wife was in her husband's forgiving arms.

It was a long time before Victoria forgot that moment when Albert locked her out of his room. A few years later, when she and her Consort had grown to be partners in every sense of the word and when she turned to her husband for help in everything she did, she realized just why he had done it. Their early married days together were extremely happy. They had only one serious problem. Victoria wanted to keep her domestic life separate from her duties as Queen. Albert wanted to be the head of his household and to share his wife's life in all its aspects. He was determined that an unpleasant poem he had heard before they were married was not going to come true. It went:

> She's all my Lehzen painted her,
> She's lovely, she is rich.
> But they tell me when I marry her
> That she will wear the BRITSCH.

Fortunately Victoria adored her husband and learned, after some sharp lessons, that he was usually right. This was a bit hard to take at first because she, as the young Queen, had grown accustomed to being the one who was always right. She discovered, to her surprise, that she could not order him around. Albert expected to be treated as her equal, and sometimes as her lord and master. And, as he was a completely faithful and devoted husband, he insisted that Victoria control the jealousy that flared up whenever he had to be politely attentive to a guest or a lady of their suite.

The Court watched their imperious and sometimes extremely stubborn monarch turning into an adoring and almost humble wife. They were amused and astonished. Because Albert believed in early-to-bed and early-to-rise they saw Victoria giving up dancing till dawn and sleeping till noon. She had always preferred London and city life, but soon they heard her agreeing with her husband that it was too noisy and dirty and restricting and that there was nothing like the joys of quiet country existence.

One battle Albert lost and it grew to be a family and Court joke. Victoria was always sure that she would be on time for dinner, and she was always late; her husband was never able to scold or tease her into promptness. One time when he had to be away he wrote her: "As I write, you will be making your evening toilette, and not be in time for dinner. I must set about the same task, and not, let me hope, with the same result."

As the happy days turned into weeks and months, the young couple grew closer together and the Queen and her Prime Minister drifted farther apart. It was a great sorrow to Lord Melbourne, but he was suddenly old and tired and perhaps it was a relief not to have to spend so many exhausting evenings at the Queen's side. It was obvious to everyone that the man was fading and, when a change in government was imminent, Victoria did not fight it.

Albert had shown her that one reason for her unpopularity at the time of their engagement was that she had favored the Whigs too publicly. The people had not forgotten her refusal to give up her women, a decision which prevented the Tories from forming a new government. They did not like her choosing all Whigs for Albert's household and they resented the fact that very few Tories had been invited to the wedding.

But the love match had started a swing back in the Queen's favor, and when she welcomed Sir Robert Peel and his Tories into power her popularity climbed even higher. But, before this happened, an incident occurred that sent a warm tide of feeling for her all over the country.

Albert and Victoria started out late one afternoon for their daily drive. They had hardly gone beyond the great gates of Buckingham Palace when a shot rang out. There, only six paces away, standing near the railings of Green Park, was a small, disagreeable-looking man leveling a pistol at the royal couple. Albert threw his arms around Victoria. "Are you all right?" he asked. "How do you feel?" The small Queen, always brave in the face of physical danger, laughed and reassured him.

Before anyone could stop him the would-be assassin

fired again, the second bullet sailing over the head of its target and burying itself in the wall beyond her. "Kill him, kill him!" yelled the gathering crowds, who now closed around the crazy man. Prince Albert leaned forward in the carriage and ordered the driver to go ahead immediately.

As the horses drew away, the Prince Consort looked anxiously and tenderly at Victoria. It was their happy secret that she would have a baby in five months and he was more than concerned. "We must return home instantly," he told her.

"No," answered Victoria, "Mother will be terribly worried if she hears of this from someone else. Let us go and tell her ourselves and then she will know we are all right." The Duchess of Kent had a home of her own now, and this thoughtfulness on the part of his wife pleased Albert. One of the first things he had done after his marriage was to heal the breach between his wife and her mother.

A month later, while the country was still seething with indignation over the attempted assassination of its Queen, Victoria's pregnancy was announced and, after some debate, Prince Albert was named as sole Regent in the event of her death in childbirth. This meant that he would act as ruler until the child came of age.

Victoria lay on her sofa as the time drew near for her baby's arrival. No woman had ever had as tender and loving a husband as her darling Albert, she thought. How wonderfully he looked after her, lifting her from her bed to her couch and then wheeling it himself from room to room during the day. She smiled as she thought of his order that no one else should be allowed this privilege; no matter what he was doing, he said, he must be sent for when she wanted him. Dear Albert!

The Baroness Lehzen, once so close to her child-charge, had gradually and tactfully been displaced by the Prince. When she suddenly appeared to have breakfast with the newly married couple on the first morning of their short honeymoon, Albert realized that, if he and Victoria were ever to have any time alone, he must take steps. So, without seriously disturbing the love between the two women, he gradually managed to convey to them that Lehzen should be allowed to return to her home in Germany. She did, and she and Victoria kept up a close, affectionate correspondence for the rest of her life.

The baby was born on November 21, 1840. It was a normal birth but it probably didn't seem so to poor Victoria. In those days no anesthetics were used to help young mothers and, as was still the custom with royalty, she had to go through her ordeal with members of the Court nearby.

"Oh, ma'am," announced the doctor in disappointed tones, "it's a girl!"

"Never mind," answered a tired but not unhappy voice from the huge four-poster bed, "the next one will be a boy."

The Princess Royal, christened Victoria Adelaide Mary

Louisa but known at home as Pussy, was a strong, beautiful infant and her royal mother was in fine health and spirits by Christmastime. It was a happy holiday season for the little family and they spent it, as became their custom, at Windsor Castle.

Letters of congratulation had come in from all over the globe and King Leopold's contained a sentence (in French) that caused Vicky to answer him rather indignantly. "I flatter myself," he wrote her, "that you will be a delightful and delighted Mama in the middle of a beautiful and numerous family."

"You cannot *really* wish me to be the Maman d'une nombreuse famille," replied his niece. "Men never think, at least seldom think, what a hard task it is for us women to go through this *very often*." It is probably lucky that she did not know then that she would "go through" it nine times.

It would still be some time before Albert shared his wife's state problems and paper work, but he was busy proving his ability by turning their extravagant and carelessly managed households into efficient, smoothly running and, as far as possible, economical ones. Many stupid formalities, continued through the centuries, had resulted in actual discomfort for the royal family and members of the Court, and the carelessness of the staff was proved by the way a boy named Jones managed to sneak into Windsor Castle over and over to hide there and watch the Queen. One time, shortly after her marriage, he hid under the very sofa on which she and

Albert were sitting. After he had been caught several times in Victoria's private rooms and all punishment seemed unavailing, he was sent to sea with the Navy. That cured him.

With spring came the change in government and the Queen had to see Lord Melbourne replaced. It was a wrench. She insisted on keeping up an active correspondence with him—and was criticized for it. Victoria sighed when she heard what people were saying. She was learning to work with Sir Robert Peel, her new minister, and she was growing to like him, but she could not drop her affection for Melbourne. Politics certainly made life difficult, she thought. "But I must not worry," she scolded herself. "I'm sure it would be bad for the new baby."

On the ninth of November, less than a year after the birth of the Princess Royal, Albert Edward arrived on the scene. What a merry Christmas it was that year for the young couple, with a healthy male heir to the throne safely ensconced in the nursery and Victoria feeling fine again. After the big Christmas tree came down and the candles and ornaments were all put away, the Queen and her Consort began thinking about the new year ahead.

"It will be busy," said Victoria. "We must set the date for Baby's christening and I must see about making him Prince of Wales."

"You have been a good little wife"—Albert looked at her approvingly—"and now that you are well again you shall have some dancing. Let us dance the new year in and, when we return to Buckingham Palace, we must plan some gay parties for the new ballroom."

"I should like to give a costume ball," answered the Queen. "My family has never given any and they sound like such fun."

Albert saw that his wife had her wish and the first costume ball, a lavish affair with the Queen masking as Queen Philippa and Albert as Edward III, was such a success that they held another later that year.

As her nursery grew Victoria was happy to turn over some of her public duties to her Consort. His speeches were very well received, but he was never able to unbend in public and the English people had a hard time growing to like him.

When fall arrived the young couple decided to visit Scotland. It was their first trip there and it was a great success. The Scots gave them such a warm and enthusiastic welcome that the good-will part of the tour was a pleasure, and when they reached Balmoral in the Highlands, where they were to have a quiet holiday, they decided it was the most perfect retreat in the world. "We must come here as often as we can," said the Queen.

It was extremely hard to settle down to formal Court life again after the simple routines of Balmoral. Albert lost all his stiff manner there and enjoyed his vacation in such a boyish, gay way that his little wife fell in love with him all over again. Their evenings at Windsor and at Buckingham Palace always bored the Consort; Victoria would not allow any conversation except the mildest small talk—the weather, the occurrences of the day, simple anecdotes. She was afraid of any discussions in which she might feel inferior and so they were not encouraged. "We are not amused" was her chilling comment on any story or bit of repartee that she felt was out of bounds.

Albert wanted to fill their drawing rooms with the stimulating people who were making history in the arts and sciences. As he was not allowed to, he made up for it by entertaining them, from time to time, in his own quarters. "I have asked Felix Mendelssohn, the gifted composer, to come and try my organ this afternoon," he told his wife. "Do come and meet him."

The two men were very happily talking about music when the door opened and the Queen, in a simple morning dress, joined them. "I'm in a hurry," she explained to Mr. Mendelssohn, "because I'm leaving for Claremont shortly. But, good gracious," she added, looking around the room, "what a confusion!" The two musicians had been so engrossed in their conversation that they had not noticed the wind from an open window blowing sheets of music all over the keys of the organ and around the room. She knelt down to pick them up and the gentlemen leaped forward to help her.

"Let me finish tidying up, Mr. Mendelssohn," she suggested, "and you play something for us."

"I will," answered the composer, "if His Highness will play first."

The three music lovers spent a delightful time together, the men playing and Victoria singing some of the guest's songs. In a letter to his mother Felix Mendelssohn wrote that Albert played "so charmingly and clearly and correctly that it would have done credit to any professional." And that Victoria sang in "strict time and tune, really quite faultlessly and with charming feeling and expression." The royal couple would have been very happy if they had seen the letter, because this was sincere praise from a professional musician—the composer of so much great music, including *A Midsummer Night's Dream.*

Another baby girl, Princess Alice, arrived in April and the hours that the Queen and her Consort spent together drawing and etching and playing duets had to be shortened. Nursery cares and political tension between England and France kept them occupied. Louis Philippe, the King of France, wanted to make an alliance with Spain by marrying his son to either the young Queen of Spain or her sister. Victoria and Albert rather wanted the Queen to marry a Coburg prince, but they felt it would be better all around if she chose a Spanish husband.

"Let us visit Louis Philippe," suggested Albert, "and keep our plans secret until it is too late for anyone to think up reasons why we shouldn't go. We'll say it is just a family visit."

The royal scheme worked very well. France gave them a warm welcome and the King took them for a delightful cruise on his luxurious yacht. Before they returned to England, Louis Philippe assured them that he had no idea of marrying his son to either of the Spanish girls. They took this good news home with them, congratulating each other on the apparent success of their mission. Albert was also pleased and proud of the admiration his wife had aroused in the susceptible French. She was at the height of her charm and he even wrote his brother about it, saying, "Victoria was lovely to look at yesterday at dinner; she had a very low-necked dress with a bunch of roses at her breast, which was swelling up from her dress."

Their worries increased the next year with unrest in Ireland. It was a poor country and the Irish themselves were an excitable people, easily aroused to rebellion. They felt a certain loyalty to the Crown, but they wanted to govern themselves and there was continual trouble between the two countries. This was one of the difficult periods and, with this problem on their minds, the Queen and her Consort found it hard to enjoy the series of royal visitors who chose this time to come to England.

The King of Saxony arrived in June, and a few days later Albert and Vicky were astonished to hear that the Emperor of Russia was on his way to see them.

"I have been told that he has some unusual personal

habits," said the Queen. "Do you suppose we can make him comfortable?"

"He sleeps on a leather sack stuffed with hay," answered Albert, laughing. "But he travels with it."

The Emperor did bring his queer bed with him and he seemed to enjoy himself immensely. He and the King of Saxony went to the races, visited some of the Great Houses, witnessed reviews held in their honor, and attended the huge banquets which Victoria and Albert planned for their entertainment at Windsor.

But Nicholas of Russia had not come to England merely for pleasure; he had several political axes to grind and he spent a great deal of time with the Ministers. It was his secret hope to annex Turkey and he was afraid that England and France might band together to prevent him; if he could prevail on England to side with him, France would probably follow as a matter of course. The result of the talks was a secret memorandum drawn up by the order of the Emperor after he returned to St. Petersburg. It was sent to England and placed in the secret archives of the Foreign Office.

The memorandum purported to be an agreement between Russia and England to maintain the existence of the Ottoman Empire (Turkey) in the name of peace, but its wording enabled Nicholas, ten years later, to allege a common understanding with England in defense of his attack on Turkey. Fortunately for Turkey, England did not consider itself bound by this paper and the Crimean War was the result.

The next important arrival at Court was another prince. On August the sixth the young couple welcomed their second son, whom they named Alfred. As Victoria smiled down on the little pink face looking up at her from its lace-trimmed cradle, she remembered her note to her Uncle Leopold about not wanting a large family.

She turned to Albert. "Wouldn't it be wonderful to be just a family? We lose so much time with the children in this Court life."

Albert sighed. "You know how I yearn for more quiet times by ourselves. It always does us so much good to go to Balmoral, but it's so far away. Do you suppose we could find a retreat nearer London? Our private budget is healthy enough now so that we could buy it ourselves. We wouldn't want to make it an extra burden for our people."

Victoria beamed proudly up at her tall husband. "I just wish our people knew what wonders you have done with the royal household expenses, too. Why, we didn't even have to ask for extra money for all those parties for Nicholas and the King of Saxony this summer."

Although the English public was not to appreciate Albert fully until after he died, their Queen's popularity was growing all the time as a result of his fine influence and their happy life together. Victoria's Ministers, however, had good reason by this time to respect him as a man, a Consort, and a power beside the Throne. He had achieved his great desire and he and his wife now worked together in perfect partnership; he was her secretary, her adviser, her mainstay. The Queen no longer saw her Ministers alone—Albert was always present, and by her wish. And he shared in her interest in foreign affairs and in her desire and efforts to further every measure at home that would improve the lot of her people then or in the future.

When, early in her reign, the Queen ordered that she must approve all decisions made by her Ministers, she established a precedent that was now making it possible for her and her husband actually to work with their government and not be merely figureheads. The days of the absolute monarch had passed in England, but the Queen's opinion carried a great deal of weight and, as she used this power for good, there was no move to take it from her.

The royal couple always needed their holidays and they found their next one, which they spent on the Isle of Wight, especially enjoyable. Albert remembered their conversation, earlier that season, about providing themselves with a holiday home and they decided that this location would be ideal. So a year later they built Osborne House there, with Albert doing the planning and designing, and they never regretted their decision. It was close enough to London, the climate was pleasant most of the time, and they could enjoy sea breezes and bathing in the summer.

The year 1845 turned out to be a traveling one. "We should accept this invitation from Louis Philippe," said Victoria. "It can't be true, but there are rumors around again about his son marrying the Queen of Spain or her sister. And I have been wondering if this isn't a good time to visit Germany. You could take me to Rosenau at last."

Albert hesitated a moment. This was the first year for some time that they were not expecting a baby and it would be a comfortable trip for the Queen. He had been home only once since his marriage and that visit had been brought about by his father's death; but, although the old castle would seem empty to him now, he *would* like to show it to Victoria.

"Yes, Liebchen," he answered slowly. "You are right. We must go to France. And let us go to Germany, too."

It was a happy trip, in the main. Rosenau was all Albert had claimed and the villagers welcomed their prince and his royal wife with a heart-warming enthusiasm. The couple enjoyed their stay there so much that it was difficult to tear themselves away from its peace and wooded beauty. But the King of France was waiting for them at Tréport with elaborate plans for their amusement, including the bringing of the famous Opéra Comique company down from Paris to play for them.

When the visit was over, Louis Philippe took Victoria to her yacht on his barge and came on board for a talk with her and Lord Aberdeen, the Foreign Minister. "The King," she wrote in her journal later, "told Lord Aberdeen, as well as me, he never would hear of Montpensier's [his son's] marriage with the Infanta of Spain [the sister of the Queen of Spain] until it was no longer a political question, which would be when the Queen is married and has children. This is very satisfactory."

It was not so satisfactory, however, when he went back on his word a year later and arranged a marriage for the Spanish Queen with a man unlikely to father any children, and followed it with that of his son to the Infanta. This ended the alliance between the two countries for some time and was one of the reasons Louis Philippe lost his throne soon afterwards.

But this was in the future. Victoria and Albert reached home to find other problems waiting for them. A potato blight was causing widespread famine in Ireland and the famine helped to bring about a change in the Corn Laws at this time. Those in favor of free trade felt that the import taxes on grain should be abolished in order to make cheaper food available to the starving Irish. It did, of course; but it also resulted in the price of grain dropping so low that the Irish stopped raising any themselves.

While this important change was being fought for and won, there was a threat of widespread war in India. The Sikhs, an Indian nation not under the rule of the British, violated British territory and declared war. The English struck back forcefully and were able to make peace on their own terms.

This would have been a hard time for Victoria under any circumstances; the fact that she was expecting another baby in May made the difficult winter even harder to bear. But, as spring arrived, the foreign news became better and, by the time Princess Helena was born, Victoria and Albert were able to concentrate on their baby, their new home that was going up at Osborne, and the usual summer crop of visitors. Osborne House was finished that fall; the Queen was in fine health and spirits again and eager to enter into a happy housewarming.

"Poor Ireland," sighed Victoria as 1846 drew to a close. "What a dreadful year this has been for them—thousands dying of starvation, and disease spreading all over. And such unhappy results for those who were able to emigrate; hundreds dying because of the overcrowded ships, and many of them carrying disease overseas. No wonder there have been so many riots in Ireland."

"On the other hand," said Albert, who was always passionately interested in the advances of science, "we can be happy over the laying of the submarine telegraph cable across the harbor at Portsmouth. Just think what this may mean someday—perhaps one across the Atlantic Ocean! And this new ether the doctors are using to make operations more bearable is such a stride forward for medicine. No, the year hasn't been all bad."

The new year, 1847, brought Jenny Lind to England for the first time, and the Queen, always eager for good music, invited the Swedish Nightingale to sing at a palace concert. As the terms of Miss Lind's contract made this impossible, she rushed to Buckingham Palace to explain her refusal in person. Naturally it was difficult to arrange an audience with Victoria, but the lovely singer, disregarding all protests of the officials at Buckingham, insisted that she must see the Queen immediately. When word of this reached Victoria she was extremely amused and sent for her impetuous caller.

"Could you sing just for me, in private?" Victoria asked after Jenny had made her explanations and apologies. The answer was yes; the Queen sent for the royal accompanist and the music began. It soon became apparent to Victoria that her accompanist, who happened to be a member of a rival theater, was playing unpleasant musical tricks on Miss Lind. So, when the singer stood up to begin a second song, the Queen quietly dismissed the pianist. "I will accompany Miss Lind myself," she announced, and happy harmony reigned.

Things were quiet at home, but the news from France was disturbing. There was no doubt about it, the people were becoming increasingly dissatisfied with the way Louis Philippe was ruling them. He had alienated England over the Spanish marriages and he consistently disregarded the reasonable demands of his people for internal reforms. By the end of the year even Louis realized that his day was over, and early in 1848, after abdicating in favor of his son, he and his wife were forced to flee the country in disguise. Despite the ill-feeling that had sprung up between the two countries, they chose England as their refuge. The people protested, but Victoria, always softhearted, gave them a warm welcome.

"They are in trouble, Albert," she rather timidly excused herself.

"I know," scolded the Prince Consort, "but you must not show them so much sympathy. Our people have not forgiven Louis Philippe for his treachery, and neither should we."

The Prince was aware, too, that it was feared in some quarters that the revolutionary spirit, which was also disturbing Germany, might infect England, but some small riots were the only evidences of it. Ireland was perhaps a bit more troublesome than usual, but in general all was peaceful.

Troubles abroad always added paper work to the Queen's agenda. During this year of 1848 Victoria and Albert had twenty-eight thousand dispatches to read, study, approve, and sign—or alter and sign. "Dear Albert," sighed the Queen, "how could I ever do all this without you?"

But helping Victoria was only part of the Prince's heavy task. He had fought for some time to better the lot of the English working man, woman, and child, and the revolutions abroad gave him a wonderful opportunity to argue for reforms. The conditions under which the workers lived and worked were unbelievable. Hundreds were dying from overwork, starvation, and diseases that ran unchecked through the slum areas, and the new machines were causing unemployment in certain groups. The necessary improvements would take many years, of course, but Albert slipped in an opening wedge at this time and hammered away at it until he died. Charles Dickens was working for the same reforms by writing novels that exposed these same bad conditions.

Another princess was born in March, their sixth child. "Let us call her Louise for your mother and for dear Uncle Leopold's wife," suggested Victoria.

This was a quieter, happier year for the royal family, although there was another attempt on the Queen's life. As Ireland seemed a bit friendlier to the Crown, it was decided that they should make a visit there and take Pussy and Bertie, the young Prince of Wales.

"The country is so poor," said Albert. "Perhaps we could visit there on the way to Balmoral and use our yacht as our headquarters. Then it would cost Ireland very little to entertain us." And so it was planned and carried out.

The royal yacht put in at Cork, Westerford, Dublin, Kingstown, and Belfast, and the Irish towns vied with one another in showing the warmth of their welcome. The people were especially delighted to see the royal children. "Oh, Queen dear!" cried one fat old woman. "Make one of them Prince Patrick and all Ireland will die for you."

The word of the good will built up reached England and everyone felt that Victoria and Albert had earned their holiday at Balmoral. Mr. Greville visited them there in September and was so delighted with their simple way of living that he described it in detail in his journal:

The place is very pretty; the house is very small. They live there without any state whatever; they live not merely like private gentlefolks, but like very small gentlefolks—small house, small rooms, small establishment. There are no soldiers, and the whole guard of the Sovereign and Royal Family is a single policeman who walks about the grounds to keep off impertinent intruders or improper characters. . . . The Prince shoots every morning, returns to luncheon, and then they walk or drive. The Queen is running in and out of the house all day long, and often goes out alone, walks into cottages, and sits and chats with the old women. I never before was in society with the Prince or had any conversation with him . . . I was greatly struck with him. I saw at once (what I had always heard) that he is very intelligent and highly cultivated; and, moreover, that he has a thoughtful mind, and thinks of subjects worth thinking about. He seemed very much at his ease, very gay, pleasant, and without the least stiffness or air of dignity. After luncheon we went to the Highland gathering at Braemar . . . we returned as we came, and then everybody strolled about till dinner. We were only nine people, and it was all very easy and really agreeable—the Queen in very good humor, and talkative; the Prince still more so, and talking very well; no form, and everybody seemed at their ease. In the evening

> we withdrew to the only room there is beside the dining-room, which serves for billiards, library (hardly any books in it), and drawing-room. The Queen and Prince and her ladies and Gordon soon went back to the dining-room, where they had a Highland dancing-master, who gave them lessons in reels. We . . . played at billiards. In process of time they came back, when there was a little talk, and soon after they went to bed.

When the vacation was over and they started back to London, Victoria smiled at Albert. "Such a happy time," she said, "and just ten years ago I was dreading seeing you and deciding whether to marry you or not!"

IX

Ten Difficult Years

"Not many couples," said Victoria, looking lovingly at Albert, "have as much to be thankful for on their tenth anniversary as we have. Our children are healthy, our country is peaceful and prosperous—"

"And we must work to keep it so. Peace and prosperity are not enough. We still have the poor to think about and help. I want our country to be a good place for everyone to live in, not just the rich and highborn."

He looked at the children playing in another part of the room. His eyes rested with unusual fondness on his oldest daughter, the Princess Royal. Young as she was, she was a source of delight and companionship already as she had inherited her father's love of good books and good talk. He frowned slightly as he looked at Bertie, the Prince of Wales. How could any boy of his hate studying so much? Well, he must just be firmer with the lad and see that he had less time for frivolity.

Albert brought his attention back to his wife. "I am well content. And I shall be quite happy if I can see that my Exhibition plan is going to go forward. I'm so convinced of its importance that I shall not spare others —or myself."

Victoria listened to him with a mixture of pride and concern. She had to admit to herself that she was a little worried about him. He had grown more than ten years older in his appearance since their marriage, as he had lost his slim figure and a great deal of his hair. He was sleeping badly and his face looked heavy and tired.

Albert's important project had been on his mind for a long time. His plan was to invite every country in the world to send exhibits to England that would, as he put it, "give a true test and a living picture of the point of development at which the whole of mankind has arrived in this great task of applied science, and a new starting point from which all nations will be able to direct their further exertions." It was a wonderful dream and a great many important people lined up beside Albert to fight the more conservative group who insisted it was too costly a risk to take.

By early 1850 the Prince had won the battle. The Exhibition of 1851 became assured and the actual planning was started. Albert had been attracted, some years before, by a large glass conservatory at Chatsworth. The man who built it was a very able person who had started his career as a gardener's boy; when he submitted a plan for a huge glass palace to hold the exhibits, it won instant approval.

Victoria marveled over the final drawings and specifications. A glass building over a thousand feet long, high enough to enclose some of the tallest elms in Hyde Park as if they were house plants, and covering over eighteen acres of ground! Why, people would come from all over the world just to see the building alone.

The royal family welcomed a new little prince on the first of May; he was named Arthur for his famous godfather, the aged Duke of Wellington. The Queen made her usual good recovery and, toward the end of August, she and her Consort and some of the children made a state visit to Scotland. They stayed in Holyrood Palace in Edinburgh. Victoria was the first Queen of Scotland to set foot there since Mary, Queen of Scots.

It was a tired family that arrived at Balmoral for a holiday. "I am glad we will have this time to rest and enjoy ourselves," said Albert to his wife. "The last few months have been such difficult and sad ones. I cannot blame you, Liebchen, for being distressed." Victoria always took the death of anyone she loved unusually hard, and that year had seen the passing of Peel, Louis Philippe, Queen Adelaide, Albert's faithful Anson, and Victoria's uncle the Duke of Cambridge. Added to that was the news that the lovely Queen of the Belgians was dying. Apart from her grief for her Uncle Leopold, Victoria felt she was losing one of her few close women friends.

The wonderful air of the Highlands helped a great deal. The Queen and her Consort returned to London in much better spirits and health. On the last day of December they had the good news that the Exhibition building was well under way and they looked happily into 1851, when Albert's dream would come true. The Duke of Wellington was with them one day when they were discussing an unusual problem that had come up concerning the huge glass building. "We are told," said Victoria, "that there are birds nesting in the tall elm tree enclosed in the Exhibition building. The committee doesn't know how to get rid of them and they can't stay as they would ruin the carpets and displays. We can't shoot them, on account of the glass."

The Duke thought a minute; then "Sparrowhawks, ma'am; sparrowhawks!" he suggested.

On the first of May, Victoria dressed herself with unusual care. Albert's big day! I must look my very best, she thought, fastening the pink watered silk dress brocaded with silver and diamonds, which she had chosen for the occasion, and adjusting the headdress of feathers and diamonds. She looked in the mirror and sighed. It was a plain, fat woman who looked back at her now; all her slim youthfulness had gone with the years and her growing family. And, although she did not realize it, the new fashion of wearing the hair smoothed back in Chinese style did not flatter her, nor did the big pagoda sleeves and full skirt help her dumpy figure. The gay, rather birdlike expression that had made her face almost pretty was replaced now with a look of severity; the mouth was usually set in a straight line.

It was raining a little at eleven-thirty when the Queen and her husband and their two oldest children started on their way, driving through masses of cheering subjects. The English people loved nothing better than to see their royal family, a prince or two in kilts and the girls in their pantalets and crinolines and hats with velvet streamers. On this special day there were seven hundred thousand spectators lining the streets and keeping themselves in wonderful order.

"Ah," said Victoria as they neared Hyde Park, "the sun!" Sure enough, the sky cleared and the huge glass palace glittered in brilliant sunshine as they passed into it.

"It is fairyland," marveled the excited family as they looked around the building, a mass of flags and greenery and flowers and beautiful exhibits. Fountains played and the air was full of stirring music. After the opening ceremonies the crowds surged over the Exhibition. Victoria and Albert were kept busy welcoming important visitors from far and near, and the little Princess Royal spent a happy interval talking to the young heir to the throne of Prussia. It was their first meeting and Cupid eyed them speculatively.

Over thirty thousand persons crowded through the Crystal Palace that first day and its success was more than obvious. "It made my heart swell with pride and glory and thankfulness," remarked the Queen afterward.

"And it is all your doing, Albert. This time you cannot make me take the credit for your cleverness as I know you do so often."

"It is quite satisfactory" was Albert's quiet answer. He was to discover later that it was more than satisfactory, even in a financial way. It made profits amounting to almost twice the sum guaranteed, and later it was moved to a permanent site and used for years until part of it burned down. The money was put aside to found what turned out to be Albert's finest memorial—a group of institutes of art and science, on the Kensington estates, which include museums, colleges, schools.

The royal family escaped to Osborne in July and from there they went to Balmoral and began planning for a larger home there, too. It would be some time before it was finished, as Albert's design called for a huge granite castle which would look very much like the castles on the Rhine, with heavy walls and turrets.

He and Victoria decorated the interior in an overelaborate Scottish style that was criticized even then. Tartans covered the walls, floors, and furniture. Anything that wasn't plaid was thistles. The tables were loaded with knickknacks; marble statues stood in every corner; antlered deer heads hung thick on the walls.

The following year, 1852, saw further changes in France. Poor France had never settled down after the French Revolution overthrew the Throne and Louis XVI was guillotined in 1793. The people tried ruling themselves for a while, then Napoleon took over; after his downfall the royal family was restored to the throne. But the people had the power and, when Louis Philippe failed them, they took over again and elected presidents to lead the government.

By this time the once-dreaded name of Napoleon was regaining its popularity, and the Little Corporal's nephew, named after his conqueror uncle, was made President of France on the first of January. He had obviously inherited the family ambition because by December of that same year he had made himself Emperor of France, Napoleon III. As France seemed content with its new ruler, England shrugged its shoulders and recognized him.

The discovery of gold in Australia that year had been the source of great excitement at home; in September the country suffered a great loss when the Duke of Wellington died. The news of his death took precedence over everything else and the whole of Great Britain plunged into an orgy of mourning. Hundreds of thousands of pushing, fainting, screaming, and crying people poured past his bier, and his funeral was the most elaborate ever seen before or since. Victoria wrote her Uncle Leopold: "He was the GREATEST man this country ever produced."

Another little prince arrived in 1853. "I want to name him for our beloved Uncle Leopold," said Victoria. "He is so much responsible for our happiness." This eighth baby helped his parents to forget, from time to time, the threat of war between Russia and Turkey. But it was obvious that the trouble was not going to blow over; Nicholas decided this was the time to strike, and 1854 saw the end of peaceful days for some time to come. The Crimean War got under way and soon spread. France declared war on Russia on the twenty-seventh of May and England followed suit the next day, as the two countries would not allow Russia to take Turkey if they could help it.

Victoria's heart was heavy. War meant grief, work, and worry for her, and death and heartbreak for many of her subjects. But her sadness turned to indignation when she heard there were rumors going around England that Albert was a traitor, in league with the Russians.

"How dare they," she cried, "after all you have done for them. You have worked for fourteen years for England; you get up at seven o'clock and begin slaving at your desk even before you have breakfast! Your every thought is for the people; you look so tired and worn and you sleep so badly—and it has all been for them. Dearest Albert, can you forgive me for marrying you and burdening you with such ingratitude?"

Albert soothed his wife, but the hurt went deep. The fact that it took public expressions of confidence on the part of the government to kill the stories, made it worse. He was apparently still a "German Prince" to the people.

The war years were sad ones. Victoria and Albert heard details of the sufferings of their army, fighting under the worst possible conditions, and did everything in their power to help. The inadequate care of the wounded was their heaviest worry and their gratitude to Florence Nightingale was unbounded. That heroic "Lady with the Lamp" organized nurses, personally braved gunfire to look after fallen soldiers in the front lines, and turned the main military hospital from a pest house into a fairly efficient sanitarium.

"I suppose," said Albert to his wife one spring day in 1855, "you know why we have been asked to invite Napoleon and Eugenie of France here for a visit, don't you?"

"Of course I do," answered Victoria. "They want us to persuade Napoleon not to go to the Crimea and run the war himself as he is threatening to do. He's had no military training whatever."

The invitation was sent and accepted. This first meeting of the two royal couples was crowned with success. England gave the Emperor and his beautiful Eugenie a warm welcome and, before they went home, Napoleon was persuaded to keep away from the battle front.

Victoria and Albert, Pussy and Bertie, returned the visit in August and it was their turn to be warmly welcomed and heaped with honors and festivities. Albert was particularly proud of the fact that everyone who commented on their public appearances in France agreed that it was his Victoria who dominated the scene, and not the glamorous Eugenie.

It was, as usual, a relief to retire to Balmoral for a

rest after the crowded schedule of the state visit. The war seemed far away, although it was still their major worry. They were having dinner quietly one evening when a messenger arrived with the welcome news that Sevastopol had fallen to the Allies after a long, bloody siege. With that city in their hands, Nicholas could not win. This meant a great victory at last, with peace probably in sight.

Albert leaped to his feet, ran out of the castle, and rushed up a steep hill to light a waiting bonfire. "Hurray, hurray, hurray!" he cheered lustily as he set it afire. Then he turned to encourage the rest of the group, who were climbing more slowly up the hill. "Faster, faster!" he shouted. "My fire will keep you warm." It was a chilly night up on that hillside in the Highlands and the merrymakers needed both the fire and the whisky bottle that John Brown, their favorite guide and servant, produced to keep them from catching cold. Victoria watched her Consort with delight. Dearest Albert! He hadn't been so gay in years. Why, he was just like the boy she had fallen in love with fifteen years before! And she joined him happily in a sort of witches' dance around the blazing signal of victory.

A short time later the royal family welcomed a young visitor to Balmoral—Prince Fritz William, the heir to the throne of Prussia. "You know," said Albert to his wife when they were alone in their room, "it is the talk abroad that Fritz should marry our Pussy. As far as rank goes, it does seem an ideal match. And personally he's the kind of young man we want for her."

"I've been thinking about it, of course." Victoria frowned. "But our people hate Prussia right now because of its neutrality during this war. And you know how much I abhor the idea of a political marriage for any of our children. I will not allow any engagement that is not agreeable to Pussy. She shall have the right to make the ultimate decision herself. She's so young, too. I do hope Fritz did not come here to court her so soon."

But the young man certainly had; he had never forgotten the lovely girl he met at the opening of the Crystal Palace and, on the twentieth of October, he asked her parents for their daughter's hand. "We would be happy to have you for a son-in-law," answered Victoria, "but Vicky herself must say yes or no. And I must ask you not to say anything to her about it until next spring, at the earliest."

Fritz intended to obey the Queen's command, but he was young and in love. One day when they were riding up a nearby mountain, he picked a piece of white heather for the Princess Royal. She had let her donkey take her a little distance away from the rest of the picnic party. Fritz handed her the heather, their hands touched, and the forbidden words came tumbling out. The little Princess's answer left him in no doubt; he had won her heart completely. After that the parents had to agree to a betrothal, but it must be kept a secret. "It cannot be announced until after Easter," said the Queen firmly, "and there must be no talk of marriage for several years."

That winter seemed a long one, with the war dragging to a close and then the difficult peace to negotiate. And there wasn't much time to enjoy that peace because there continued to be serious troubles abroad. The year 1856 passed quietly, then in the early summer of 1857 the ghastly Indian Mutiny occurred. It was a short but violent uprising of native troops, who turned on their European rulers, massacred everyone within reach, and set fire to all the buildings. It took much bloody fighting to restore order and, before that was accomplished, the British soldiers were guilty of avenging their comrades and their families in an equally barbaric fashion.

What actually caused the mutiny is not certain. Ruling India, with its millions of inhabitants, was a difficult job for the handful of British assigned to it, especially as they had to use native troops to keep order. Some say it was the general policy of the administration that brought about the mutiny; others that it was specific acts on the part of the government. Whatever the reason, the result was a reign of death and horror—one of the heavy penalties of acquiring and holding a vast and rich empire.

With these acts of terror going on in the background, the royal family was busy with happier things at home. Victoria had her ninth baby in April, the Princess Beatrice. On the fifth of May, Albert opened the great Exhibition of Art Treasure at Manchester and was enthusiastically received. The Queen glowed happily when she heard the good report. "Perhaps my stupid people will finally appreciate you," she said.

On the nineteenth of May the forthcoming marriage of the Princess Victoria and Prince Fritz was announced; on the twenty-fifth, Victoria officially conferred the title of Prince Consort on Albert. It had been merely a courtesy title until this time.

The next day the Queen bestowed, for the first time, the Victoria Cross, the most highly prized decoration in Great Britain, on some of her brave war heroes. England had never decorated its soldiers and sailors before, perhaps taking their valor for granted.

The rest of the summer and the fall slipped away and the new year found the palace in a bustle of excitement. Pussy's wedding was planned for January the twenty-sixth and it was to be an elaborate affair, as befitted the rank of the young couple. London and the palace itself were full of visiting royalty; magnificent gifts flooded in from all over the world. The staff was kept busy with balls, dinners, and musical parties, and places for eighty or ninety persons were set for every meal in the state dining room.

Some months earlier, Lord Clarendon, the Foreign Minister, had said to the Queen, "I hear Berlin thinks the wedding should take place there."

Victoria bridled indignantly. "The assumption of its being too much for a Prince Royal of Prussia to come over to marry the Princess Royal of Great Britain in England is too absurd, to say the least. . . . Whatever may be the usual practice of Prussian princes, it is not *every* day that one marries the eldest daughter of the Queen of England. The question, therefore, must be considered settled and closed."

The day of the wedding was beautiful and sunny and the Chapel Royal at St. James's Palace, the same chapel in which Victoria was married, was redecorated for the occasion. The Queen stood waiting for the entrance of the bride, and keeping an anxious eye on her young family clustered around her; the boys were dressed in their best Highland kilts and the little princesses wore matching gowns of pink satin trimmed with Newport lace.

As Pussy appeared on the arm of her father, the Queen's heart jumped with a mixture of emotions. How beautiful her daughter looked, in her lace veil and the silk dress with its deep, off-the-shoulder neckline and its long, heavy overskirt! Then her critical eye passed approvingly over the eight bridesmaids, all in white tulle with wreaths and bouquets of pink roses and white heather, the courtship flower.

As the familiar service began, Victoria thought back to her own happy day. I feel, she thought, as if I were being married over again myself—only more nervous. She looked tenderly at her Consort. I have not that blessed feeling which I had then, which raises and supports one, of giving myself up for life to him whom I love and worship—then and forever.

When a child marries and goes away to another country one cannot help feeling a mixture of happiness and sadness. Prince Albert sat down at his desk after he had said goodbye to his daughter and wrote her a loving note. "My heart was very full when yesterday in the salon you laid your head on my breast to give vent to your tears. I am not of a demonstrative nature, and therefore you can hardly know how dear you have always been to me, and what a void you have left behind in my heart."

There was sadness in that letter, but there was certainly happiness in the short cable that Victoria and Albert received from the proud, new husband: "The whole royal family is enchanted with my wife."

The next year was a quiet one. And in 1860, a year now considered one of great British prosperity, Canada grew insistent in its demands for a royal visit. "Let us send Bertie," suggested Albert. "It is time he tried his wings; perhaps it will increase his sense of responsibility. I feel we have failed with the boy, Victoria, and yet I have tried in every way to turn him into a thoughtful, serious young man."

"We must carry on as we have begun," she answered, closing her mind to any possibility that their methods could be wrong. "There could be nothing better than to train him to be exactly like you."

The Prince of Wales, who had spent a miserable childhood and a lonely boyhood under the too stern and shortsighted guidance of his parents, surprised everyone by taking Canada by storm. He had a natural charm and an ability to make friends that was one of the most important qualities a future king could have. It was a great triumph for the nineteen-year-old boy, and all England was proud of him.

The Queen and Albert welcomed in the new year of 1861 rather wearily. The duties of state were heavy and the problems of foreign policy seemed more worrisome than ever. If Victoria had realized what sorrows this year was to bring her, she could not have faced it.

The first blow fell in March. The Duchess of Kent, who had always been a healthy woman, fell ill and, within a few days, died. Victoria gave in completely to grief. Her husband and children tried to comfort her, but it was many grim and depressing months before they could congratulate her on being herself again.

The Prince had always had to battle with his wife's tendency to be overemotional. She was apt to make crises out of ordinary occurrences, and any serious discussion between them was hampered by bursts of tears. He had finally written her a note, suggesting that any time she had something to say to him that might be too disturbing for words she write it to him instead.

One day that autumn Victoria was working at her desk when Albert entered looking tired and angry. She dropped her pen. "Albert!" she exclaimed. "What is wrong?"

The Prince Consort dropped heavily into a chair and covered his face with his hands. "It's Bertie," he groaned. "I must go up to Cambridge immediately. I—I hate to tell you this, Liebchen, but the boy is in some trouble over a woman." His expression was grim and heart-broken. "Oh, Victoria, if he is going to be like Ernest and my father, I cannot bear it!"

Victoria tried to comfort her husband, but her heart was as sore as his and her anger at her son even greater. Albert made the trip, settled the distasteful problem, and returned home exhausted. His wife watched him dragging himself through the long, busy days and tried to persuade him to rest a bit more. November was cold that year and Albert couldn't seem to keep warm. They were at Windsor and, even though he sat as close to the fires as possible, he could not escape the drafts.

The Prince did not want to worry his wife, but he certainly was not well. He was haunted by vague pains and aches that grew worse each day, and a cloud of depression settled over him that made it extremely difficult to keep up appearances. But he forced himself every morning to rise at his usual early hour, put on his long brocaded bathrobe with its velvet collar, and take his place at the writing table he shared with Victoria.

Seven o'clock on the first day of December found him at work on the draft of a very important dispatch. The

War between the States had broken out in America that spring and England felt, correctly, that it was a problem that must be handled at home. Unfortunately the word had just been received that a federal man-of-war, the *San Jacinto*, had fired on an English mail and passenger ship named the *Trent*. Its captain had boarded the *Trent* and demanded the surrender of four Southern emissaries who were among the passengers.

As Albert drove his trembling hand over the paper in front of him he thought with horror of what it might have meant if the Foreign Office had already sent off the dispatch that lay on the desk before him. It demanded redress and apologies in a manner that would almost inevitably lead to war between Great Britain and America. He altered a phrase here, deleted a sentence there, and finally turned the message into one that would put out the fire instead of adding fuel to it.

It was done at last and the Prince Consort's last ounce of strength seemed to go with it. But Victoria was expecting him to review some of her troops with her and he managed to get through the ordeal of dressing for the ceremony. It was a warm day but, as he stood beside his wife, even the long, fur-lined coat that he had decided to wear seemed inadequate. I feel, he thought, as if someone were pouring cold water down my back.

By bedtime it was obvious that Albert was ill and the Court physician was called to his bedside. "You don't need to worry, ma'am," he reported to Victoria, "it's just a low fever and all he needs are rest and care."

Lord Palmerston, the Prime Minister, was the only person who showed any real concern. "Please, ma'am," he begged the Queen, "call in more doctors."

"I don't think it is necessary," answered Victoria. "Our physicians assure me that he is gaining every hour and I can see myself how much he is improving."

Victoria and her doctors were wrong; Albert was not getting better. He tried getting up on December the sixth and was soon back in bed, weaker and with a higher fever than ever, and unable to take any nourishment. The only thing that soothed him at all was to have his daughter Alice read to him. There was a great deal of typhoid fever round Windsor at this time and the doctors finally admitted that the Prince had the dread disease. "But he has only a light case," they assured the Queen.

Again Lord Palmerston pleaded for more doctors and they were called to Windsor. Perhaps they could have saved Albert if they had been summoned sooner, but it was too late now. Poor Victoria! She spent hours at Albert's bedside, cherishing every lucid word and still convinced that he was getting stronger every day. She wrote constantly to her Uncle Leopold, always assuring him that the invalid was on the mend. "I do not sit up with him at night as I could be of no use, and there is nothing to cause alarm . . . we have *never* had one *unfavorable symptom*."

While the Queen was writing hopeful bulletins to King Leopold, the Princess Alice was growing more and more concerned over her father. She heard him murmur "Dear little woman" to her mother and saw him slip back into delirium. She watched him rest his head for a moment on Victoria's shoulder. "It is very comfortable so, dear child," he said; but his eyes were too bright, his face so thin.

"Mamma," she whispered, "don't you think we should send for Bertie?" The news of Albert's illness had brought some of the other children to the castle, but no word had gone to the Prince of Wales at Cambridge.

Victoria's face tightened. "No," she answered bitterly. "It is his fault that his father is ill and I don't want him here."

On the morning of December the fourteenth the Queen rose early and received one of the doctors at six o'clock. "I have no hesitation in saying that the Prince is much better" was his completely erroneous report. "There is ground to hope the crisis is over." At seven she went to the Prince's room, expecting to see him looking stronger.

"The room had the sad look of night-watching," she wrote later, "the candles burnt down to their sockets, the doctors looking anxious. I went in, and never can I forget how beautiful my darling looked, lying there with his face lit up by the rising sun, his eyes unusually bright, gazing as it were on unseen objects, and not taking notice of me."

The morning passed. The Queen walked on the terrace at noon, but the sound of a gay tune being played somewhere nearby was too much for her and she burst into tears and returned to the sickroom. The doctors knew now that the Prince's lungs were filling and there was nothing more they could do. "We are very frightened," they told her, "but don't and won't give up hope. The pulse keeps up. It is not worse."

As the day waned, even Victoria saw that there was a sad change and Alice was glad she had taken matters into her own hands and sent for Bertie. The Queen slipped out of the room for a moment to control her grief. Albert had spoken to her—"Good little wife"—then moaned piteously.

The Prince was unconscious now and his breathing grew more difficult. Alice sent for Victoria and tried to prepare her for the inevitable. The grieving family knelt around the bed; the Queen dropped to her knees by her husband's side. She heard his feeble breaths with the feeling that she was in a horrible dream. This could not be happening. Albert could not be leaving her. No, he could not! She loved him so; she needed him so!

The great castle clock struck the third quarter after ten and Albert left her. The Prince Consort was dead.

X

The Widow of Windsor

Victoria sat at her desk trying to control her overpowering grief long enough to write her Uncle Leopold. As he had been the first to receive a letter from her as Queen, engaged girl, and bride, so he would hear immediately of her sorrow as a widow. "My *life* as a *happy* one is *ended!*" she wrote, stopping to dab ineffectually at the tears that streamed down her plump cheeks. "The world is gone for *me!* If I *must live* on . . . it is henceforth for our poor fatherless children—for my unhappy country . . . and in *only* doing what I know and *feel* he would wish."

King Leopold answered her letter in person, his heart breaking for his bereaved niece and from his own sorrow at losing his beloved nephew. He took Victoria in his arms and tried to comfort her. "My child," he said tenderly, "you must go to Osborne at once and leave all the final arrangements to me. The services would be too much for you to bear. And if you should catch this horrible fever we might lose you, too."

The Queen finally agreed. "But I must help you plan the services first," she said.

It was a sad task; but she found some measure of comfort in doing it, especially in choosing the music. She turned to the final prayer which is always offered up for the reigning monarch. "Here," she commanded, "where you pray for my 'long life and happiness'—I want that changed to 'long life with honor.'" She buried her face in her hands. Happiness, she thought. There will be no more happiness for me.

Victoria retreated to Osborne and let sorrow have its way. She gave in to it completely, staying almost entirely in the beautiful, comfortable suite of rooms that she and Albert had planned together and in which they had spent such happy hours. She stood in their sitting room, in the rounded bay with its windows looking down over the terraced gardens to the blue waters of the Solent; but her eyes were blinded with tears and she saw nothing. She wandered to the twin tables, set side by side, where she and her husband had worked together on state affairs; she touched his pens, his inkwell. His umbrella stand stood nearby, with his canes and umbrella in their places. Where was he?

She went into the big bedroom and flung herself on the large double bed, her hand clutching the pillow where Albert's head had rested. From now on, she thought, she would do only what Albert would have wanted her to do—every word, every action, would be weighed first with his approval in mind. She roused herself slightly. These dear rooms, everything, shall be kept just as they are. She pondered a moment. I shall have a picture of my beloved on his bier and hang it here on the headboard over his pillow. Then he will still be beside me. And I shall have a little silver plaque made and placed on the footboard where I can see it, with the dates of the first and last time we shared this bed." She noticed that the silk pocket for Albert's watch still hung on the silk-covered headboard. "I must remember to put his watch in it and wind it every night."

In the days and weeks and months that followed, Victoria's children and friends were distressed to see that nothing mattered to her except details and plans concerned with her husband's death and his memory. His clothes must be laid out every night, hot shaving water provided and left in his dressing room. Memorials of every kind were under way: an elaborate mausoleum, monuments, his biography. The sculptor who executed Albert's marble effigy, to rest on his tomb, was summoned. "I would like you to do mine now," the Queen told him, and made arrangements to hide it and keep its existence a secret. She did not want an aged model of herself to lie beside Albert, in the event that she lived to be an old woman.

Those who loved Victoria tried desperately to interest her in outside things, even in a walk or a drive to the Swiss Cottage playhouse where her children had played and learned to cook in a miniature kitchen with tiny equipment. Finally, in despair, they sent to Balmoral for her favorite pony.

With the pony came John Brown, a brusque, forthright Scot who had served first as Albert's gillie in the hills of Balmoral, then gradually had taken a place there as the Queen's personal attendant. She had always liked his way of talking to her more as man to woman than as servant to queen, and she decided to keep him with her now as part of her year-round household. He persuaded her to ride around the grounds of Osborne in her pony cart; he looked after her; he scolded her; he even bullied her. He became, in fact, so indispensable that she allowed him too many liberties. She overlooked the times he drank too much whisky; she closed her eyes and ears to the criticism and gossip that grew up concerning them.

When the news of Albert's death was announced to the people of England, they hoped that the Prince of Wales, who had become extremely popular with the public, would take his father's place at Victoria's side and share her responsibilities until the time came for him to ascend the throne as king. Articles to this effect appeared in all the leading newspapers and Victoria read them with mounting indignation. She had not forgiven Bertie for his part in Albert's illness; it would take years and a narrow escape from death by the same typhoid fever that had killed his father to restore him to his place in his mother's heart.

The Queen stood before her advisers, who had just made it clear to her that they, too, thought Bertie should take his father's place. Their arguments had made no impression on her. She and Albert had planned their son's education and that plan would be carried out to the letter. "I want this public announcement made," she commanded, her mouth set in grim and stubborn lines. "The Prince of Wales will carry out the completion of his education and make a tour of the Eastern lands."

The Empire accepted Victoria's decision with disapproval, and waited for her to conquer her grief and come out of seclusion. Years passed. Still the word came that the Queen could not resume her public duties. She went from Windsor to Osborne to Balmoral and back to Windsor again, refusing to set foot in London. Only when there was a public ceremony connected with Albert's memorials did the people have a glimpse of the small, dumpy, heavily crepe-veiled figure. All her charms were gone now; the once birdlike mouth was a severe line, turning down at the corners. The pretty blue eyes were red-rimmed and seldom free from tears. The light step had slowed under the weight of grief and crepe, and the delightful, clear voice, rarely heard in public these days, was usually choked with emotion.

The world, of course, was not standing still. America fought its War between the States and, in England's political arena, two champions were working their way to the top. Benjamin Disraeli, of the Conservative Party, a brilliant, unusual, charming Jew, was one of them.

The other was William Gladstone, a Liberal, a great man and a fine administrator but a man without humor or tact. These two were to take turns as Prime Minister during a large portion of the rest of the Queen's reign and, in their opposite ways, to have much influence on her. Victoria began by disliking and distrusting both of them, as she often did with her Ministers. Gladstone remained the only Minister who never won her favor; Disreali, using flattery and charm, became one of the important men in her personal and public life.

There were changes in the royal family as the years passed. Engagements, marriages, babies, deaths, including the Queen's beloved Uncle Leopold; but neither the happy nor the sad events made too much impression on the cloistered widow. Bertie won the hand of beautiful Princess Alexandra of Schleswig-Holstein-Glucksburg and, when the Danish bride arrived in England in 1863 to marry the Prince of Wales, the people welcomed her with unparalleled enthusiasm. She was lovely; she was warmhearted; she had an exquisite face and figure, and a charming simplicity of manner that was irresistible.

Victoria paced up and down her study trying to decide on plans for the wedding ceremony. She knew only too well that her people wanted her to end her seclusion with this happy occasion, and to let them have a great royal wedding in London with all the pomp and circumstance that should surround the marriage of the heir to the throne of Great Britain.

"Oh, Albert!" she mourned. "If you were only here!

What a happy day it might be. But I am sure you would want the children to be married here at Windsor so that I will not be put to any strain." And so the plans were made and carried out and a wave of disappointment and disapproval swept over the country. It was a brilliant ceremony in the Chapel Royal at Windsor, but Victoria, looking like a plump black raven in her heavy mourning, watched it from a small adjoining room.

The Prince and Princess of Wales came back from their honeymoon and Alexandra took upon her graceful shoulders the burden that Victoria had dropped, holding Drawing Rooms, making public appearances, entertaining. Time passed and it was obvious that Bertie could not have chosen a more satisfactory wife. As well as performing her social chores, Alexandra went successfully about the task of filling the royal nursery with both princes and princesses. And, although Victoria still kept him out of state matters, Bertie began to show such a knack for diplomacy that the Ministers sighed unhappily over his wasted talent. His popularity grew daily and the people of Great Britain, increasingly impatient with the Queen's retreat, began to clamor for him to be made Regent.

These rumors reached Victoria and she answered them with royal indignation. "I work myself to death over the affairs of state," she said, pointing to the overflowing baskets and boxes of papers that filled her study. "And I am not well. Send out an announcement that my health makes it impossible for me to appear in public. My people *must be made* to understand my situation."

The Queen's Ministers had struggled through six long years since Albert's death. She still insisted on seeing and approving everything the government did, and Albert was not there to shorten, clarify, explain, and counsel. Her advisers took this task upon themselves as well as they could, but the Prince Consort was missed not only by Victoria. As Disraeli said, "With Prince Albert, we have buried our Sovereign. This German Prince has governed England for twenty-one years with wisdom and energy such as none of our kings have ever shown."

Added to the difficulty of coping with a woman who had lost touch with the world, was the fact that she was always hard to reach. Windsor was not far from London; but Osborne was several hours away and she spent a great deal of time there and at Balmoral, more than forty-eight hours from town. A king, acting as Victoria did, might have lost his throne. Luckily for her, a woman inspires more sympathy and patience.

Finally, in February, 1866, Victoria agreed to open Parliament for the first time since Albert's death, but she did it unwillingly and grudgingly. She drove up from Windsor and arrived at Buckingham Palace nervous and tired. I am exhausted already, she thought as she turned with distaste from the food awaiting her. They should not have asked me to do this.

The carriage drove through the streets and, as the

bands played, the Queen found it difficult to hold back the tears. The people cheered her, but their loudest hurrah's were for the Prince and Princess of Wales. "I feel as if I might faint," worried Victoria as she entered the big Parliament buildings crowded with Members. She walked to her throne and, as she wrote later in her diary, "all was silent and all eyes fixed upon me, and there I sat alone."

The Lord Chancellor read her speech for her, as she had refused to do it herself. It was soon over, and the stiff, silent, crepe-draped figure rose, bowed slightly, kissed Alexandra, and slipped quickly out of the room.

It was an unsatisfactory appearance, but it *was* an appearance and it was a small crack in the ice. She continued to refuse to take up residence at Buckingham Palace and entertain as she should, but she agreed, from time to time, to having visitors at Windsor for lunch or even overnight. This was an improvement, but it was not good enough. Criticism became general again and, in 1867, she sent out a bulletin that her health made it impossible for her to appear in public. She had a bit of rheumatism at that time, but the real trouble was that she had grown shy and uncertain of herself.

From the moment she ascended the throne until the day her Consort died, Victoria had had the constant comfort and support of a man who devoted himself to her and her interests; first it was Melbourne, then Albert. In February of 1868 a new Prime Minister took up the reins and stepped into the vacant place at the Queen's side.

Disraeli, with his eyeglass and his odd, sensitive face surmounted by a curl of dark, silky hair, was a man with a keen understanding of women. He approached the problem of the cloistered Queen in a new way, flattering her, showering her with notes and gifts, winning her affection and trust and, most important of all, making her feel like a woman again.

This first term of Disraeli's was a short one; he was Prime Minister for ten months only. A general election brought William Gladstone into power and Disraeli's "Faery," as he called Victoria, found her new Minister stern, cold, and unsympathetic. Gladstone called her pleas of ill health "fanciful ideas." He told her flatly that she was neglecting her duties.

Victoria was deeply angry. "How dare Mr. Gladstone distress me with his impossible demands?" she fumed. But she found herself taking her place in public more and more and, although she would not yet admit it, almost enjoying it. She gave in to her Prime Minister's insistence, but she never forgave him for it.

When the political wheel took another turn and Victoria had the happy task of welcoming Disraeli back as Prime Minister, it was like stepping out of a cold room into a warm one. Disraeli now had time to finish the work he had started and which Gladstone, in his different way, had helped along. He turned all his carefully calculated sunshine on the Queen and she blossomed contentedly. Buckingham Palace held no terror for her now and she took up the burden of Drawing Rooms, garden parties, and large breakfasts with a cheerful heart. Her fiftieth birthday rolled round and she smiled at her household. "I feel like a new woman," she said.

Life was suddenly worth living again. After almost ten years of seclusion, it was stimulating to be back in the world. She found the music of a man named Arthur Sullivan well worth encouraging (sometime later she would sing songs from *Pinafore,* which he wrote with Gilbert), and a short time before that great author's death she had a long private talk with Charles Dickens. It was very sad that Victoria had by this time lost her thoughtfulness for other people; she kept the ill man standing during their whole interview. She was, in fact, so much the Queen now that she never moved to a chair if she wished to sit down—she just sat, knowing someone would be watching and would place one under her in time.

Victoria drove out in her carriage often now, opening bazaars, visiting hospitals, attending functions. Her heart swelled as she heard the cheers that greeted the sight of her vehicle, for she knew she was regaining the love of her people. They had their Queen back and they were glad of it; they knew that although she still mourned her husband, living in a forest of mementos of their years together and spending the anniversary of his death each year at Windsor near his tomb, it was not the fanatic grief of the earlier years. Victoria traveled abroad now, to visit children and grandchildren and to spend time in sunnier climates.

In 1876 Disraeli saw to it that she had a great personal satisfaction; she became the Empress of India. When he died in 1881, the loss of her supporter, friend, and courtier was hard for her to bear.

June 20, 1887, rolled around and Victoria went from the breakfast table to the secluded garden behind Buckingham Palace, with her diary in her hand. "The day has come, and I am alone, though surrounded by many dear children. . . . Fifty years today since I came to the throne." She looked around the garden where she had been so happy with Albert and thought that even nine children, forty grandchildren, and a growing group of great-grandchildren did not make up for his absence.

This was her Golden Jubilee Day, celebrated all over the vast British Empire, and she dressed herself with special care for the triumphal procession to Westminster Abbey, where a service of thanksgiving would be held, The gown was black, as always, but her bonnet of Spanish lace sparkled with diamonds and her somber dress was relieved by the Garter and the Star of India; she had refused to wear crown and robes. It was a happy but tiring day, clouded, as always, by Albert's absence. "I sat *alone,*" she wrote. "(Oh! without my beloved husband, for whom this would have been such a proud day!) . . ."

The next ten years passed with the country flourishing in the sun of prosperity and progress. The personality of the old Queen mellowed. She was still dictatorial and sharp; she could still send her fifty-year-old son into a cold perspiration by her frown; her chill "We are not amused" could still reduce the unfortunate teller of a slightly questionable story to the depths of embarrassment; but, as a rule, she was mild and calm and even stopped underlining words in her letters. Her household looked after her with deep love and loyalty and, unlike that of her children, the love of her grandchildren was not tinged with fear, and her great-grandchildren took intense delight in being with "Gangan."

John Brown was gone now and she would be attended by other kilted servants and by attentive East Indians in their native costume. Edward, the Duke of Windsor who would have been Edward VIII if he had not abdicated to marry unsuitably, never forgot watching his great-grandmother, in her white tulle cap, black satin dress, and shiny black boots with elastic sides, have her breakfast in a little revolving hut mounted on a turntable, so that it could be faced away from the wind. These shelters were fascinating to the children, as was the bathing machine at Osborne—a sort of house on wheels that could be drawn out on the sloping pier and down into the water so that the curtained porch would rest in the water, and the occupant be safely and modestly immersed.

Victoria still toiled over her desk, but the reins lay slacker now. She was enjoying an Indian summer; her health was good enough to make traveling a pleasure. Reading over all the papers to be signed was more difficult than it had been, but her secretary copied every-

form of photography, the daguerreotype, had been invented when she was born.

Victoria turned her attention back to the happiness of the moment, bowing and waving to her excited people. A great country, indeed, and a great day.

There were not many years left for Victoria now and life became increasingly difficult. One granddaughter was the Tsarina of All the Russias and, although the British Queen dutifully stepped back to allow her descendant to precede her through the doors at Balmoral when the Tsar and his wife were there, Victoria derived no joy from the royal couple's visit. There was no meeting of minds, no sympathy between them. What heartaches there were in having children married into almost every ruling family in the world—what strains were put on love and loyalty! She thought with distress of her favorite grandson, Pussy's oldest boy, who had become the Kaiser of Germany. Now that Germany had consolidated into a powerful nation, young William was showing signs of becoming a greedy, overambitious ruler, and his grandmother found it hard to justify some of his actions.

War came to the Empire during the Queen's eightieth year. It was hard on the old lady to suffer through the heartbreaks and tensions of more bloodshed, for she was tiring now and her eyesight was failing; but her sympathies were with her people in South Africa who, though twenty times more numerous than the Dutch Boers there, were not allowed any voice in their government. Her people, she was told, were overtaxed, were allowed no freedom of the press, could not meet or present petitions.

British troops from all over the world were mobilized to meet the emergency. It was a hard war, full of defeats and despondency. Victoria was a tower of strength, inspecting troops, encouraging their wives, cheering her Ministers, and her fat little hands were always busy knitting for the soldiers. When it looked as if defeat was inevitable and reverses and compromises were discussed, the Queen spoke up firmly: "Please understand that there is no one depressed in this house. We are not interested in the possibilities of defeat; they do not exist."

Victory was won at last and those brave words were put aside to be used again in 1939, when Britain needed them even more.

By the fall of 1900 Victoria was increasingly miserable. She managed to move from home to home, but she was sleeping very little, rheumatic pains were constant, and the cataracts on her eyes made reading almost impossible. She dictated her journal now and its closing pages were a sad account of her approaching end, which came on January twenty-second. Her memory began to fail and those near her sent for her children. Those who could come, gathered at her bedside at Osborne. The Kaiser, who was to be England's great enemy, rushed over from Germany but was almost too late. He entered the room and went over to the bed for a last embrace. She roused herself for one word—"Bertie," she said, and died. Her grieving children brought her wedding veil and draped it over her, as she had requested earlier. There she lay, a bride again, with her beloved Albert's picture beside her. The long years of separation were over at last.

Bibliography

Sitwell, Edith. *Victoria of England,* Houghton Mifflin Company, Boston, 1936.

Strachey, Lytton. *Queen Victoria,* Harcourt, Brace and Company, New York, 1921.

Creston, Dormer. *The Youthful Queen Victoria,* G. P. Putnam's Sons, New York, 1952.

Bolitho, Hector. *The Reign of Queen Victoria,* Collins, London, 1949.

Watson, Vera. *A Queen at Home,* W. H. Allen, London, 1952.

Gurney, Mrs. Gerald. *The Childhood of Queen Victoria,* Longmans, Green & Co., New York, 1901.

Flexner, Marian W. *The Young Victoria,* M. Joseph Ltd., London, 1939.

Benson, E. F. *Queen Victoria,* Longmans, Green & Co., New York, 1935.

Benson, E. F. *Daughters of Queen Victoria,* Cassell and Company, London, 1939.

Jerrold, Clare. *The Early Court of Queen Victoria,* G. P. Putnam's Sons, New York, 1912.

Jerrold, Clare. *The Married Life of Queen Victoria,* G. P. Putnam's Sons, New York, 1913.

Lee, Sir Sidney. *Queen Victoria: A Biography,* Smith, Elder & Co., 1903.

Oliphant, Mrs. *The Domestic Life of the Queen,* Cassell and Company, Limited, London.

The Life and Times of Queen Victoria, Cassell and Company, Limited, (4 vols.), London, N.D.

Benson, A. C., and Esher, Viscount. *The Letters of Queen Victoria,* John Murray, London, 1908.

Esher, Viscount. *The Girlhood of Queen Victoria;* A Selection From her Diaries, Longmans, Green & Co., New York, 1912.

Graham, Eleanor. *The Making of a Queen,* J. Cape, London, 1940.

Buckle, George, E. *The Letters of Queen Victoria,* Longmans, Green & Co., 1926-28.

Victoria, Queen. *Leaves From the Journal of Our Life in the Highlands,* Harper & Brothers, New York, 1868.

Bolitho, Hector. *The Prince Consort and His Brother,* D. Appleton-Century Co., New York, 1934.

Fulford, Roger. *The Prince Consort,* Macmillan, London, 1949.

Martin, Theodore. *The Life of His Royal Highness the Prince Consort,* Smith, Elder, & Co., London, 1875-80.

Jagow, Dr. Kurt. *Letters of the Prince Consort,* John Murray, London, 1938.

D'Auvergne, E. B. F. *The Coburgs,* J. Pott & Company, New York, 1911.

Grant, Daniel. *Royalty at Home,* J. S. Virtue and Co., Ltd., London, 1894.

Cecil, Lord David. *Melbourne,* Bobbs-Merrill, 1954.

Windsor, Duke of. *A King's Story,* G. P. Putnam's Sons, New York, 1951.

Strachey, Lytton and Fulford, Roger (editors). *The Greville Memoirs,* Macmillan & Co., London, 1938.

Ellice, Jane Harriet. *Some Memories of the Queen's Childhood and Marriage,* Cornhill Magazine, London, 1897.

Law, Ernest. *An Historical Guide to Kensington Palace,* 1923.

Rowse, A. L. *Royal Homes Illustrated,* Odhams Press Ltd., London, N.D.

Parsons, Julia Stoddard. *Royalty in the Nineteenth Century,* Humphries

Beavan, A. H. *Popular Royalty,* Sampson Low, Marston, London, 1897.

Davenport, Millia. *The Book of Costume,* Crown Publishers, New York, 1948.

Encyclopaedia Britannica, 11th Edition.

Index

ABOUT THE AUTHOR

MOLLY COSTAIN HAYCRAFT was born in Toronto, Canada, but moved to Philadelphia with her family when she was nine. Her father, the well known author Thomas Costain, was then editor of a leading magazine, and so she grew up in a world of writing and writers. When her education was completed, she came to New York to work for a literary agent until her marriage to Howard Haycraft, author, editor and now president of H. W. Wilson Co., a library publishing house. With such a background and an inherited love of history, it was no wonder she herself decided to write. Mrs. Haycraft is the author of a number of historical biographies and novels for young people and adults.

thing for her with a broad-nibbed pen and dried his work in a special small copper oven so that the ink would stay black and clear.

The years pass quickly for the old; before Victoria knew it, it was time to listen to the plans for her Diamond Jubilee. Sixty years a queen! All the royalty of Europe had gathered round her to celebrate the Golden Jubilee; but this one was to be more of an Empire Day, with the premiers of the dominions and colonies assembled to honor the occasion.

It was a busy, happy, and tiring few days for the old lady; but she never faltered, even finding the time and energy to describe the festivities and her gowns in her journal. For the big dinner she wore a dress with its front covered with gold embroidery, especially worked in India; for the great procession, the following day, she was dressed in "black silk, trimmed with panels of grey satin veiled with black net and steel embroideries." Her bonnet was trimmed with creamy white flowers, an aigrette, and some black lace.

The open carriage was waiting to begin the six-mile drive through the London streets to St. Paul's Cathedral, where an open-air thanksgiving service would be held. The route was lined with millions of cheering, singing subjects. Before she stepped into the vehicle, Victoria pushed an electric button that telegraphed her message of gratitude to every corner of her Empire. "From my heart I thank my beloved people. May God bless them."

As she rode along, escorted by troops from far and near, her thoughts were, as usual, with Albert. How proud he would have been of the great prosperity that had come to their country—its wealth had tripled and its trade was six times what it had been when she came to the throne. Australia, with its neighbor New Zealand, Canada, and Africa had grown into great colonies and India was a source of power and riches. Someone had computed that one out of every four square miles in the world flew the British flag, and one out of every five persons alive was Victoria's subject.

She sighed. Dear Albert! So many of his dreams had come true. So many of the reforms he had worked for had come about. The wonderful growth of the railroads, the substitution of machines for slow, backbreaking manual labor, the development of the steamship lines, the prison and hospital reforms, the progress in clearing up bad sanitary conditions, the bills that had been passed to improve the lot of the working people, and the reform bills that gave more persons a voice in their government—all these things would have made him so happy. She remembered how sorry he was when the Atlantic cable that Cyrus Field, of America, had laid across the ocean in 1858 had failed, after a few successful months. Well, the one he substituted in 1866 was a success! . . .

If Albert had been at his wife's side till the day she died, he would have seen her using a telephone, recording her voice on a phonograph, and being photographed by a motion-picture camera—and not even the simplest